12 · 9 · 2019

us

so

much :)

Christine

x x x x

The Lonely Poets' Guide to Belfast

The Lonely Poets' Guide to Belfast

A poetry and resource guide visiting Belfast's people and places

With an introduction by Maureen Wheeler, Co- founder of The Lonely Planet Publication

Published by the New Belfast Community Arts Initiative

First published in Belfast, Northern Ireland in 2002
The New Belfast Community Arts Initiative
Unit 4, Clanmil Arts and Business Centre
3 -10 Bridge Street, Belfast BT1 1LU

ISBN 0-9540662-3-5

Printed and bound by Easyprint
This publication was funded through the support of
The Arts Council Lottery Fund and Belfast City Council

CONTENTS

Contacts

Things to Do and See

Touring

North Belfast

South Belfast

FOREWORD

The day I left Belfast my mother said - "You won't come back" - I protested that of course I would, perhaps after a year or maybe two, but as the plane took off I found myself hoping that she was right, Belfast was so small and the world was so big, I wanted to explore it all.

Travel had always been my dream, and I am very lucky because my dream came true. But the thing you discover about dreams is that you never come to the end of them, one dream leads on to another. Just as all the best journeys never end, because the more you travel the more you discover how much there is to see, the world actually gets bigger, not smaller, and there are always new roads to explore, higher mountains to climb and other seas to cross. And most often the destination is less important than the journey.

My mother was right, I never came back to Belfast to live. My visits were few and fleeting, I had real excuses, it was so expensive to return, I had so much to see, and my life was elsewhere. But some years ago family circumstances brought me back for a longer stay, and as I wandered around the new Belfast and spent time with old friends and family, so many memories came flooding back. I felt as though the ghost of my younger self was walking alongside me. I kept seeing fleeting glimpses of old friends in much younger faces, and found myself wondering "could that be....?" So many memories of myself as a child, a girl and a young woman returned. It was as though the person I had been and the person I had become had finally come together.

I realised how much it meant to me to keep a connection with the place where I had grown up and the people, my friends and family, who really know who I am.

For this reason I accepted a role with an Australian television channel as a presenter on a travel show. I agreed to do it, although I find the process of being on television unbelievably tedious, on the condition that we would do a segment on Northern Ireland. So several months later the crew, the producer and I landed in Algergrove. We had only a week and we were to cover Belfast, Enniskillen and the Antrim Coast Road. I was worried about everything, - what if it rained for an entire week? What if the crew hated it? What if we couldn't find anything really wonderful?

Well the weather was gorgeous, every day was sunny and hot, Belfast looked wonderful, we got fantastic shots from the top of the Hilton across the Lagan, at night we visited great restaurants and pubs and the people were always friendly and helpful. The Antrim Coast Road shimmered in the heat, looking like a dream of Ireland, and in Enniskillen the peace of the lakes, the green of the fields, interspersed with many coloured wildflowers looked like a painted backdrop for Finian's Rainbow.

I was very proud to show these Australians around, to answer their questions, to see Northern Ireland through their eyes and realise how wonderful it was. It also brought home how much had changed in the more than twenty years since I had lived there. When I left Belfast I landed in London to a completely different world. Back home just about everyone I knew looked like me - there were no African faces or Asian faces or even other European faces. I once had an American cousin visit me for a while, and I was very gratified at the stir he caused with his 'strange clothes and ways'. Northern Ireland was a very insular place, food was always recognisably meat, potatoes and vegetables. One of my first dates in London invited me out for a pizza and I had no idea what that was – a food? A film? An immoral suggestion?

Now of course, Northern Irish people travel widely, I remember walking down a steep track in the Himalayas a few years ago and hearing a familiar accent coming up the hill towards me, sure enough, a family from Newtownards. And they are used to many different people, in a restaurant in Bangor, County Down I met a young Indonesian waitress and was very pleased to show off my very limited Indonesian in front of my brother.

Yes Belfast has changed, in some ways it is unrecognisable, I often find myself wandering lost looking for an old landmark and then realising that of course, it has gone. But so much remains, if not in the cityscape then with the people. Some of my best friends in the world live here, my family too and I find myself fitting in, like slipping your foot into an old shoe and realising that how well it fits and how comfortable it is.

I miss the old jazz clubs by the markets, the serious, contentious discussions of my youth, in bars, when politics, music, literature and poetry were being discovered and explored. I believe we are formed by where we grow up, and although I may not always know where I am going, I know where I come from, and I am very proud to be from Belfast, which is why I was so thrilled and honoured to be asked to write this foreword.

Maureen Wheeler, Co-founder of Lonely Planet Publication

poems are sticks and stones

or crumbs

like the ones Hansel saved from his mouth
to drop on the forest floor and point them home
- barren walls, the wrong side
of the door, the roof letting in
and it's better you don't return
better the crumbs feed birds

and some are stone
like the ones Hansel gathered
before the door was locked —
drawing you back to cup each moon in your palm and
pocket them all 'til they rattle the whole song
out as you rap on the door

and some are sticks
like the ones Gretel gathered for kindling
to fuel their way out of woods and cages and
ovens, a circle of light
to ward off the beasts
howling for the moon of your sweetness

and sometimes words
the ones that don't come tripping off the tongue
but fly like sticks and stones or crumbs
from the hand of a vagrant —
in stories that cannot be told completely
old as the river that carries us with them

to catch the moon in water

Ruth Carr

EDITOR'S NOTE

The title came through consultation with local writers and literary folks, including festival organisers and local library boards on National Poetry Day on October 4th, 2001: "If we are thinking primarily about Belfast as place...people...communities...emotions...good/bad things...North, South, East, West - What about a sort of 'Lonely Poetry' Guide to Belfast?" With this idea as the signpost the Poetry in Motion project set out to meet some of Belfast's people and places through the words of its citizens.

One year on and worlds have changed, the world has shifted. Writing continues as a witness to the universe of the poet. For the contributors, whether it is a full time commitment or a first time experiment, they will occupy the space in the world of readership, as poets. For readers outside the North this publication is a window on a collective creative voice of Belfast, a rare book from Northern Ireland. As a community arts project it is the continuation of a city-wide dialogue with writers and the public and is the follow-on publication to "You Can't Eat Flags for Breakfast." In that book, we asked poets, politicians and the public to submit work based on their experiences and hopes for the future of Belfast. Looking back on it, for me, it was an exercise of visioning inclusive political leadership. This book articulates further stories from this city in its process of transformation.

Travel and poetry occupy similar points of view that encompass a widening of perspective, openness to new experience and a sense of movement and "flux". The movement of people, ideology and associated emotions have underwritten the history of this city for centuries. What is clear is that there are many in Belfast who practise a unique craft, privately, who are at the centre of a shared city and are not alone in a vision of a creative process that is the liberation of the spirit through language. It is with great appreciation to include a foreword from a spirit as liberated as Maureen Wheeler: positive, confident, following a path of her own choosing. The Lonely Planet publications, of which she is the co-founder, have been very helpful and have given brilliant introductions to cultural experiences covering every corner of the world.

This book is a result of the tremendous activity and interest in writing in Belfast. Sometimes it can be difficult to grasp all that is happening at grass roots level; although this book could not be a comprehensive review I hope there will be a sense of "person and place" as well as a greater definition of the activities happening within it. At the back of the book there is an appendix that may be helpful to local writers - as contact details are sometimes "in motion" please confirm all details before attending an event to avoid disappointment.

I would like to thank our partners, the Arts Council Lottery fund and Belfast City Council, for making this programme possible. Also, I would like to thank the members of the selection panel who made difficult choices in selecting the work within this publication: Sinead Morrissey, Brendan Hamill and Robbie Meredith.   Medbh McGuckian, Ruth Carr, Niall McGrath and Chris Agee informed the basis of the programme through their series of workshops, forums and constructive feedback sessions.   John Brown, Martin Mooney, Rebecca Hunter, Jo Egan and Joe Sheehy were consistently open for friendly chats and suggestions. Also, thanks to Ruth Carr and Padriac Fiacc for their poems and support. Throughout the project I was ably assisted at various times by Kate Duggan, Eilis Haden, Nalan Salih, Tracey McCauley and Rosemary Jenkinson. Ultimately, all credit for this publication lies with its authors, as well as all the 140 poets who contributed their work to this process.

The Poetry in Motion project reaches the people of Belfast through two elements: a workshop series and publication for young people at school and, for the adult public, workshops, exhibitions, and publication opportunities. The role of the poetry project was to facilitate a dialogue of the written word and the human spirit. This public project encouraged local writers and potential writers to send poems based on a idea of "A Lonely Poets' Guide". After the submission process what remains is to represent the work back to the public from which it came: through poetry on the Citybuses and taxis, as public art work and through publications.

I am grateful to the following organizations who hosted workshops and events during this summer programme: the Northern Whig pub, First Step Drop-in Centre, Suffolk Library, Ballyearl Leisure Centre, Arcadia Café, Linen Hall Library, Grace and Goove Café, Skegoneil Library, Whiterock Library, Postscript Café, 174 Trust, Walkway Women's Centre, Falls Road Library, Bookfinders Café.   Finally, Miriam Rodgers accompanied many of the workshops in an effort to document the events through photographs.

Josh Schultz, Poetry in Motion (public) project co-ordinator

Facts about Belfast

THE TEXTURE OF WATER

When we first came to this new place
by the Lagan I did not know much about rivers,
but now I am learning to assess
the changing texture of the water.

I can see how the weir's loom provides
the water's warp, and how the wind
reaching up the channels from the lough
passes the weft crosswise under its ebb and flow.

At times it is a strong brown river,
tugging tree limbs and discarded plastic bags
like half remembered things,
and cold rain purls the plain of its surface.

But the best days are like these,
when the river is a mirror made of old glass,
broken, then healed by a grebe's wake, and
at the edge of the wharf, a heron keeps a steady watch.

Carolyn Thompson

OUR FUTURE

Oh Lagan!
   Take my voice.
Let it soar above the sounds of wind and rain.

May your current help it slip in and out of rocks.
Reeds cannot muffle it mud won't dampen its confident note.

Bear it away to fall on ignorant ears,
so they can hear,

its clear tone

showing we're
a resilient people.

Betty McAlister

A GARDENER QUESTIONS TIME

He straightens up stiffly into the soft spring breeze and leans on his spade
The newly turned earth at his feet is rich and damp in its recent revelation
Deeply he breathes in its sweetness
and allows his gaze to wander over the garden
The smooth, unflawed greenness of the lawn pleases him
His eyes reflecting each regimented shrub and weed-stripped flowerbed
The reward of his love labour

Beyond the fencing, outside the limits of child-noisy suburban gardens
and graffiti-scarred streets
Like old, best friends the familiar mountains gently rise,
ignorant of the tribal divisions fomenting at their foot
In the gardener's mind questions begin to take root
What dramas had this land seen before the red bricks blossomed
And the tendrils of the city had snaked ever more close
towards the mountain horizon?

Did the path of the marching men cross this plot
as they took the road to fight and die
Brother against brother for elusive freedom?
Did the clay beneath his feet hold memories of the tread of tenant
families shouldering humble possessions
Carrying their old world with them from bothy and hovel to start afresh in
the far-off New World?
Could the land he now worked have felt the barefoot
tread of weeping women and
Ghost-gaunt children as they struggled to survive
in the famine-scoured fields?

Had this ground ever shaken to the trampling of startled beasts
and the swift, strong strides of fierce warriors and their kinfolk
Returning from the raid and driving their neighbours' herds before them?
Or could this be a part of the pilgrim trail
touched by the feet of the great saint
As he journeyed the island to bring the Druid-serving people the Word of
his God?
What tears would Patrick now
shed if he could see the fruits of his mission

Blighted by hate, division and destruction, death and despair
in the shadow of his Old Church?

The questions have trickled into his mind like a stream,
nourishing his imagination
He smiles to himself at that moment plucking
an answer like a flower from his thoughts
He is at one with this land and as much a part of its history
as those who have come and gone before
The riddling of his mind completed, he turns back to tend his charge
His own small patch of this land's time

Joyce Macartney

BELFAST
(For Maureen)

Stirrings of rain on tree and flower,
Then sunbeams between the jumbled clouds,
And Saturdays see the bustling crowds –
God grant us grace to heal the scar.

Brendan McDermott

WHAT LIES BENEATH

A thriving, busy, bustling town
Prosperity of a kind,
In those fine new buildings
And cleaned up streets
Interdenominational night- time revellers,
Called to pray at the altars of entertainment,
Throng the brightly-lit thoroughfares.
City of Culture? Perhaps
But don't scratch the veneer
Too deeply
Nor far beneath the surface
The cholera pit in Friars Bush.

Olivia Butler

Facts for the Visitor

BELFAST'S PARTING KISS

It was my last day in Belfast after Christmas and the New Year. I was doing a bit of shopping, rummaging through January sales, absorbing the sights, smells and feel of hometown streets to do me for another while, as I returned into exile. Bedford Street had been bombed the night before. Windsor House, the tallest building on the island, cried its windows out. I gazed, dazed, in silence, beheld chaos.

I went looking for a pair of jeans when the tell-tale white-tape cordoned off the street. A van abandoned outside River House. This was the Belfast I knew when I lived there - a parting memory, a nostalgic touch, like an old lover's kiss, I thought. I went around to Waterstone's book-shop, the nearest haven of peace I could find, to try to escape the anticipated harrowing sound, shrugging off my home-town. I was browsing through the Irish book section when the blast came.

I was surprised by the muffled sound. This new-fangled Semtex stuff must be more subtle than the earth-moving gelignite of my Belfast days? I thought it was only the flirting move of the army's controlled explosion. My legs trembled a little alright and most people's heads turned slightly, acknowledging the blast, almost politely. No one said a word; then they went back to flicking through books. I rushed for the bus and an evening flight, shrugging the embrace of this, my birthplace.

Bernard Conlon

24

INTERFACE

I crouch in the hallway of Queen's main library
rifling Mayakovsky's 'How Are Verses Made?'
watching the bonfire lights of Belfast city
and the wormhole darkness that breeds riots

where bombs smash windows, detonate
on fireside rugs, displace family photos
shatter a Sacred Heart above another fireplace
blast holes in walls, puncture sofas.

A clatter of children scream in their beds
crying for a different bedtime story
and I know how revolutionaries are made
in this war that's not a war.

Deirdre Cartmill

PIG IN THE MIDDLE

Three floors up I was cleaning the windows
Of my aunt's flat.
The heavy chamois for washing
And muslin for polishing wrung out
My arms like bell ropes, as from inside
She sang out orders and complaints.

Balanced on the sill, I reached around the
Open end of the sash to scrape off the
Sticky remains of the label - the windows
Were new and plastic, double glazed
To keep out the noise.

Stopping to silence the clanging
Muscle bells in my arms, I looked across to
Green hills over the neighbour's
Red white and blue painted gable.

A soft day.

Through the Saturday shopping morning
A flute band drummed its insistent
Presence over the parading traffic's
Dissonant hum.

The March rain, as predictable as
Every other march, began to offend the
Polished order of the windows, and I closed the
Sash to keep it out.

The fluting drums faded behind the
Double skin of glass.

I watched the purple-coated cortege ignore a
Give way sign and turn the corner
To complete their circular route,
And disband where they had begun,
An hour and three hundred years before.
I lifted my eyes to the soft hills
Where the overhanging
Banner of cloud menaced
Green and red and blue and gold and white,
And the rain drummed harder.

And I could hear my heart's pulse
Beat in my temple to a different measure,
As the snare-drum of the past rallied
Another age of innocence to beat its path to
Traditional mass sacrifice and
Oblivion.

George Sproule

THE OTHER SIDE

He lived in 22 I in 95
His father Sean his mother Bernadette.
He said 'Holy Mary Mother of God
Pray for us sinners now and at the
hour of our death'. I did not.

I could not see him, the wall blocked my view.
His side green, white and gold, mine red, white and
blue.
I could not see him, the wall blocked my view.
I could not see him, but then I did not choose to.

Linda Collins

REFUGE

In this bus-shelter, broken
Glass strewn around my torn
Trainers, feeling every chill
Of the icy blast blowing up

From Belfast Lough, in and out
Of this fragile frame, through a young son
Of Loyalism, on the face of it, unaware
That there can be no real refuge there.

Gavin Hawthorne

QUEUE

What spectacle do they queue to see, and say you have gone to a
better place,
with no more pain that you are free.
Where is this place where you rest at last, that states our love is
past, when here and now it is to me in the present.

What spectacle do they queue to see
They who dunk biscuits in tea, in china cups that don't belong to
us, say they are sorry
for my loss while staring at the pattern of the carpet.

What spectacle do they queue to see
They who stood in the baker's shop where a craving for cream
buns fed you and me, who
stood again to catch first sight of you, the sight that hijacked my
heart.

What spectacle do they queue to see
They who uttered ooh and aah on the day, original sin was wiped
away and again when
you received the bread of life and your eyes of the summer sky shone.

What spectacle do they queue to see
They who line the path of deep dark earth where crocus burst
awake lie trodden in limbo,
they who carry your frostbitten body that friction fails to warm or
embraces excite.

What spectacle do they queue to see
They who stand on the edge of the ravine as the volcano erupts,
they who you call friend,
with hearts of stone dig the bed where you must sleep forever.

Christine O Reilly

This poem is dedicated to my nephew Christian O Reilly

ESCAPOLOGY

Only the tips of icebergs show,
testing the specific gravity
ratio of hate, weight,
to a given memory.

Dogmas bark in the night,
leaving the ship of state.
Enough lifeboats for everyone,
this time.

Attempting the great trick,
life after death.
Seeing beyond ourselves,
the need to practise escapology.

Iain C. Webb

BELFAST FOR THE MILLENNIUM

The city in the grey mist squats
Its buildings slump and sigh and rot
They're throwing money left and right
Making us a tourist sight
So they can show us to the world
Like some copper-faced cosmetics girl
who, from a distance seems to please
But you see there's nothing underneath
And all your shiny phalluses
will never hide the calluses
The "make it look nice" plan will fail
Because people who live here are just too real
Old hatreds which are festering
won't stop because of your building
Investment figures are very impressive
but people here just aren't that progressive
I know that we need something here
but its not a big hotel, I fear
We need some new inhabitants
if progress is to stand a chance

So Belfast was a dowdy spinster
Here comes big business to save her
He slaps on make-up, much too much
fake tan, blue eye-shadow, just a touch
He dyes her hair, buys her a dress
He wants his friends to be impressed
This dinner party's quite a big deal
He hopes that Belfast will appeal
He gets her drunk but he stays sober
so it's easier to bend her over
And when we're well and truly used
he'll take back the dress and shoes
And with the morning comes the truth;
old Belfast, she's so very loose
They'll walk away once they've made the money
find some new land for milk and honey
We just carry on as before

Wishing there was something more
than one night stand investment plans
Wishing for that old gold band
of commitment with a long-term view
with something there for me and you

Her children leave her every year
and they all say there's nothing here
Well maybe if you stayed around
you could start to smooth the ground
cause the ones who always seem to try
never seem to realise
that only we can make it work
not dark blue suits and shiny 'Mercs'
Cause only we know what we need
All we follow's our own lead
The crane begins to slowly move
Builders come in threes and twos
They don't care that the money pours
until the tourists come no more

As though Belfast's back streets we trudge
we see the make-up start to smudge
And the shiny big hotel we got
now sits with all the rest and rots

Robert Rainey

THE BELFAST AMERICAN

A captive recluse, with an audience of one-legged volleyball players.
Why do you throw vodka over an already soaking bridge covered
sombago?
Stop running from mistakes that only Gay Byrne can account for. Sure
Paddy Black never fought no British convention.
Your confession box lies just open, as if you thought it was a shoe
menders podium.
You are richer than a bitch in a convent full of policemen.
Are you Irish or Óirish? From Pennsylvania or Troon? Do you live
with your ma, or are you a female priest on marijuana?
Stop knotting in parables of Jesus and June. Stop pretending of love
than protruding in cloudy smudges of lust!!!!!

David Cullen

Getting There

OUT OF THE CELLAR

Not an old city, really.

Still though it seems to wheeze,
Reluctant and complaining
Like a cross, smoky old man

Climbing a flight of steps
Up and out and into
A half-remembered world
Of daylight and God's own fresh air.

Colin Hamilton

TRAMS

I remember the trams,
  The rattling, groaning, grinding trams,
Their trolleys and their iron wheels,
  The ting of the conductor's punch,
The tickets blue or red or white,
  The old trams red, the streamliners blue,
Trundling along their shining lines---
  Yes, I remember
      The trams when I was young.

William Dalzell

MUSIC LESSON

I am seven years old.
The window is filled with my face,
Watching for her return. The rain,
Globed like semibreves, is a page of music.

I know nothing but deafness
At the end of those fists,
A fist's sforzando
Pummelling the white keys black.

The window is a stave
Ringing all the captive notes' ransom.
They cling to their bars,
Too afraid to leave.

The conductor is so black and white,
He sees only right and wrong.
I am his wrong.
You are the conductor,

Waving your arms to the rhythm
Of your rage.
I stand here, mute as a page,
Waiting for the cadence

Of a chair in the air
Or another broken door
And the tiny, awe-filled applause
Of rain against the window

Before she comes home
To the Grand Finale.
How well you know this music!
You heard it often as a child

Falling beautifully on the walls'
Decidedly deaf ears.
You grew to love the black and white,
You knew then where you stood

With him, your father.
Every silence must be filled with a concerto,
A tug of war,
And I, your echoing hiatus,

Must be filled with the din
Of your scars
That cry out their unheard melodies
At the end of your muffled wrists.

The window wells up with tears.
There is a change of key.
You behind me,
Beating time with a belt.

Carolyn Jess

The city road lived on its nerves
edgy brick tensed its walls
chimneys sneaked out timid smoke
windows darted their glass in the shadows
parlours took cover behind net curtain

a child sat upright at an upright piano
a front door jumped to the turn of a key
Beautiful Dreamer peppered the hall.

Una Woods

The way distance thins
invisible time heard
the faint dog-bark
like one thing
happened

Una Woods

FOREST DRIVE

Imposing, established evergreen
Space for development
Saplings shaped, placed for show
The shelter of their canopy impervious,
except by accepted route

We pass through

The broadleaf forest
Another season's growth
Nurseries full, flourish
Dreams of the aspirant
push higher from reach

We look

Exposed, dreary plantation
Outgrown
For seedlings the outlook bleak
Storm ridden, skeletal forms
too many to sustain

We stare

Stark clearing
Unwanted tangle of branches, stumps remain
Green shoots strangled by briar
The rot, the decay removed
The journey renewed?

We hope not to break down.....

Mark Cooper

LAUGHING IN A FOREIGN LANGUAGE

I can laugh in seven languages -
Self-taught -
All more authentic than my native speech,
Its cynic's bray hoarsened by smoky politics,
The predictable cackle of opinion.
My younger tongue knifed asides
Double-edged in lethal obsidian,
That fractured existence blamed
On an accident of birthplace,
A harsher climate.

Multilingual mirth is a hotter proposition –
Untamed –
A travelling stranger, counterfeit with wine,
Glee glazed by holiday nights, bazaar days.
With head thrown back,
Hair unfettered like a palomino,
My throaty cadence shocks shoppers
When I laugh in outlandish accents,
Unafraid to be ecstatic - even in Cornmarket
In a downpour.

Lindsay Hodges

THE WRECKED CAR TELLS ITS STORY

I never questioned any of it –
different hands on the wheel,
scorching up roads I'd never seen before,
the numbers inside me going through the roof,
fiercely exultant, behind us the screech of sirens
falling away as we jumped
the central reservation, for a minute
I thought I was flying, then as we crashed the barrier
I felt myself somersault, hands wrenched away, the wheel
aimlessly spinning, bodies tumbling out of me –
I could hear them groaning. Cursing. The spurt of a match.
Different hands again pouring the petrol
and I was a ball of flame, of pain and delight
till the plastic and rubber was all melted off me, my bones
not gleaming as I'd expected, but charred and black.

For days I smouldered. The stench would choke you. Then
shouts and whoops as they hoisted me over the fence –
the rip of spikes on metal – juddering
over stones, ricocheting off trees, no flesh on my wheels
to cushion the blows, roof buckling, doors wrenched off
until at last I came to rest in the grass
between the railway line and the drifts of nettles.

No hands will touch me now. Only the hiss
of aerosol sprays. Kicks. Laughter. Matches
flaring but there's nothing left to burn.
I begin to question, but my story's so small –
there were many fires in the city that night, I was one –
perhaps the only one to end like this,
camouflaged, rusty brown, among the beech leaves.

Here let me squat for ever, barely disturbed
by the surge of trains - a hoot and a rattle, then gone –
the occasional snuffling of dogs, the thrashing of branches,
the scolding of robins and wrens, the ticking of fibres
as they snap and settle in the debris within me,
the prancing feet of magpies that poke about
in my dried-up entrails, looking for something shiny.

Janet Shepperson

TAXI

rain reverberates on the roof of the car
inside the
three jobs a day man
sighs
straightens
stretches
bent
back
bowed in a
6 day a week crease

taximan
barman
driver for the handicapped

outpaced by the cost of living

inhalation rasp as he sits

"you're gonna kill yourself" his wife says

He knows
she lies awake into anxious nights
feels her
touch
delicate on his thick veined hands

he worries too
never says.

when he was a young man
he dreamed he'd retire by 40
witness to his father's death
from working.
He was a fine large man, his father
fine breeds in his blood
who he remembers as being

"always too tired to play"

dead
by the time they straddled adolescence.

He is himself
already over 40
nicotine stained
heavy from a no time to exercise life
still mortgaged
still children, at college, to support

He recalls their wide eyed first days
him choked with pride
long lost dream realised.

He shifts
winds the window
to allow in a slice of air

Inhalation rasp as he remembers
himself

son
lover
husband
father
worker always worker

He drains the cup of gone cold coffee
restarts the engine

"where the hell have you been the radio rasps
we've been trying to get you for the last 15 minutes"

He sighs
makes no reply
feels ready
for a day off

Jani X

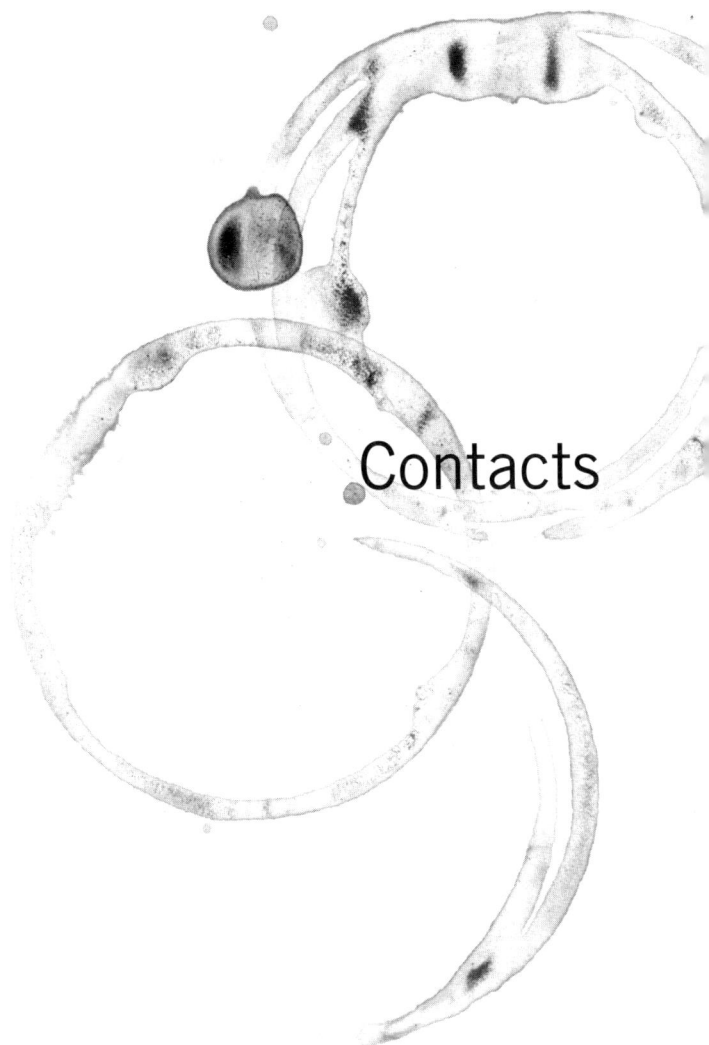

Contacts

FOR ALL MOTHERS

Here's to all mothers from one mother to another.
This poem is for all mothers who have sat up all night
with sick babies in their arms, saying "it's ok baby mummy's here".
Who have walked around the house all night when their babies wouldn't
stop crying.
This poem is for all mothers who have shown up at work
with milk stains on their blouse and nappies in their bag.
This poem is for all mothers who gave birth to
babies they shall never see and the mothers who took
those babies and gave them homes and all their love.
This poem is for all mothers who have yelled at their kids
while shopping and slapped them in despair as all tired
two year olds do then hated yourself for "losing it".
This poem is for all mothers who taught their children
to tie their shoe laces before they started school and
for the mothers who opted for velcro.
This poem is for all mothers whose head turns automatically
when a little voice calls mum in a crowd.
What makes a good mother anyway? Is it patience?
compassion? Or the ability to nurse a baby, cook the dinner,
sew a button on a shirt all at the same time, or is it the heart?
This poem is for all mothers who have tearfully
placed flowers and teddy bears on their children's graves.
This is for all you special mothers who are and those
who could not be one.

Eileen Burke

RED

We sat on the bottom stair, my sister and I
Doctor rushed past with black bag.
Our baby is in there,
We giggle and creep up a few stairs.
Neighbour making tea coaxed us down.
Bath water running,
We tip toe up
Peep around doorframe.
Water gushing, sheets swirling,
Spongy soled slippers engraving
Red bubbles on floor.
The scene held us there.
The smell,
The red smell.
Softly speaking,
Siren screeching,
Siblings searching.
Mammy missing.
Part of her never came home.

Christine O Reilly

NARCISSI

Each Mothers' day a dozen of these small-faced blondes
Pucker up from their vasial collar, dominating the room
With their dense incense. Their pale abstracts shimmer
Like surfaces, eager to echo all that catches their eye.
They are so telling of the giver, I am told, they orbit
Their own reflective diorama. I can tell they know yearning,
Their hundred watts hooded up from the surface they long to burn.

I've given them to you every year since using their petals
To stop the blood that flooded the nail-hole in your sole
When my six year old hands could no longer hold it.
I had never touched anything so alive, so full of its own
Trajectory. I thought of a candle lending its flame from
Stem to stem until its own soul waned blue.
Fearing you might die, we both cried.

They have the charm of starlets. I imagine them congregated
Here to audition for that big break, or perhaps a beauty pageant,
Clinging to the mirrored surface. An aura of ambition bleeds
Around their clam-edged corona, the hazy outline of lights
Underwater. I think of mermaids caught in the fisherman's
Net, dazzling him with their beauty until he sets them free.
Their long green tails gestate below the surface, going nowhere.

Their mouths are not the shade of daylight but Jack Lanterns
Uplighting the face, etching the years in shadowed contours
Around the eyes like whorls ringing in a tree. They are too
Brazen to know anything of tact. I spent all these lines
Searching for complication, anything but simplicity! They are
Projectile as a lens inhaling all our blind spots, each one plotted
At her thirty degrees like the face of a clock, impressing each

Hour I become more like you upon the memory of their stems.
They would have you believe they were young too, once,
They loved as I do, lost as I did. They assure me I will find,
Once more. When you held on to your own mother's loosening
Grip they gathered by the hospital bed and beamed like lighthouses
As the darkness tugged her free, joyous as souls about to be born,
Occupying the sudden emptiness with their plump, radiating
aliveness.

Now I see their necks bowing to the gravity of the surface
Peering up at them for answers. Their hemmed-in legs seem to be
That guided path we must forge in untrespassed, umbilical
terrain, pushing through the darkness to the brightness at the end,
Stopping then only to look down as you do at me, finding
Your own face looking awkwardly, amorphously back,
An eye filling up with its own reflections.

Carolyn Jess

home in time for the funeral

I would visit him on Thursday
and he would welcome me with a fire
and treats for tea
I would sit at his feet and watch
as he slowly cut tobacco
pressed it into his pipe and lit up
with the first puff his chin would stick out
as he watched the smoke float up
and disappear into a stain on the ceiling
he would tell me yarns
as I stared into the fire unleashing my imagination

I grew up and went away with loving memories
his were taken bit by bit
he grew confused with our new age
and angry at his surroundings
where once ships docked
now yachts anchor
living was sliced of meaning
and words packaged
he'd laugh at Made in Taiwan labels
as factories were bulldozed
his head would shake in his
one room pensioner flatlet at our thinking
or lack of
then he'd gaze over the new image ghetto
towards the mountains
and rest his eyes on an old friend
I hugged him and beneath my fingers

felt but a bundle of bones
his eyes were like a winter's sky
I pressed tobacco in his palm
it was an empty gesture
smoke alarms is all he said
an invite for a pint was taken up gladly
with the suggestion of Malloy's
where hearth and fire could be found
I was waiting he said and you were
a long time in coming

Jacqueline Dickson - Thompson

GENEVIEVE

Or my grandmother,
Who ironed sheets
In the dark place under the stairs,
Her long slender fingers
Smoothing the starched linen
While she whistled
Between clenched teeth.
Her wispy hair in clips and she
Was still tall then.

But who could remember the nightmare,
Once, as a young woman,
Exploding out of the house
Into the deep night, tearing
Like a wild thing through the dark grasses
Hissing at her feet,
Her bare heels banging the dusty earth,
Her mouth open,
Her teeth open,
Her breasts steaming
As the men tracked her,
As they cornered her,
Her red eyes
Unfamiliar
As they carried her home across
The metal echo of her own
Scream,
As they laid her down softly
On a bed of medicine,
Tutting and worried
But unseeing,
As she rose the next day
To continue the rest of her life
Tame.

Morna Finnegan

PAIN NEEDS NO BATTLE

To my room he'd come in the
night shadowed in dreams
of mother's stupor
we'd play.
I'd get hurt, always
to cry disturbed mother's dream
pain needs no battle.
In the pulse of night
we'd play
in the absence of mother's
awakening
cradled in his strength
I hurt.

Maura Rea

This morning in the steam room
I imagined how I would feel
If you were to be killed in a car crash,
And suddenly vanished from my life.

I felt sick.
But I didn't turn away,
I asked myself what emotion it was?

And it was guilt.

This evening I thought of
Your face,
And a longing so hard
As to allow me to rest against it
Came,
That I began to cry.

I imagined our baby girl.
I imagined our 9 dogs,
All brothers and sisters.
I imagined the wild cats
And the soft eyes of our cows,
Heads together,
Talking in a language we lost centuries ago.

I love you.

You're the most vulnerable person I know.
I keep thinking the world is going to hurt you.
The world you love so much.
If you knew how many times I have cried
Just thinking about you.

I'm afraid we will grow old having not
Grabbed this life.
We will be dead soon.
I don't really mind that;
I've been dead before after all,
And it didn't do me any harm.
But maybe this is the only chance
I will have to live in this world.
Maybe this long white shell that houses me,
And allows me to touch and smell,
And move like an animal,
Is a once only gift.

I want to know what it feels like
To watch your belly swell.
To put my ear down,
And listen to the big bang.

Richard Irvine

NADIA

White coral shells smile from a sandy beach
A rock half exposed trails dreadlocks of black crinkled
seaweed
Stopping short of a vast expanse of sea
It was morning, fresh virginal sand
Still an undiscovered paradise
With a yet unfounded social scene
Yet to develop as the day wore on
This inlet limited to home waters
With all the potential of a full roaring tide

John McKittrick

Things to Do and See

BELFAST BAP RAP

I wanna soda and potata
and a crusty bap
I'm gonna get it now
from the corner shop
I'm gonna fill up me pan
with a pound o' lard
and put it on the ring
while I'm whitening the yard.

I got a sausage and a chop
a bitta vegetable roll
it's hard to lose weight
when you're outta control
I'll put an egg on, it's healthy
and if I'm gonna die
make sure my belly's full
with an Ulster fry.

And when I go to heaven
I'm gonna take the pan
and a bottle of Bushmills whiskey
for the spirits and yer man
and on that judgement morning
when I'm floating round the sky
I know I won't be living
but dying for a fry.

Pat Turner

MY WORDS

I want to stand
    On Napoleon's Nose,
High above the city,
    And shout my words
Through a massive megaphone,
So that everyone can hear
    And know what I have to say.

I don't want to see my words
    Bound and contained
Within a thin, sterile book,
    One copy on a shelf in 'Dillons',
That no one's going to see
    Or want to buy.

I don't want to bind my words
    I want to yell them.

Mark Kennedy

A POETRY READING IN BOTANIC GARDENS

Outrageous fronds of foliage, like green giraffes
browsed through leaves of poetry, read under glass.
Never had the Palm House heard such language,
condensing like thunder,
syllables blowing up a storm,
staining your jacket with phrases.

Sultry in profile, a hothouse flower,
by dusk your fingers were cerulean
as the thermostat drooped –
even the prayer plant curled its tongue,
teeth chattering at an outside world
too quick to vegetate, unmoved.

Still we lingered at the recitation,
accompanied by percussive droplets
drooling from the luscious canopy.
I wanted to describe the bliss of being
dripped upon like this – instead
found myself lost for words.

Lindsay Hodges

MADDEN'S BAR, CASTLE COURT

They're like mushrooms spreading, fanning out in the damp, woody room.
Pinky brown caps in the shade like beer-heads sprouting,
Their breath fugging the windows.
Across warped joints of ceiling planks the light spawns ripples
The snug wood swallows harsh words into a hum.
Heat grows, crucibles, steams the room into a Palm House
A girl branches her body over a boy and her lips bow heavy as pink blossom,
Dousing, drowsing his face with honeydew.
But suddenly the fire exit is opened for the coolness
And fermenting rings plump up again, gills ruffling
And they slurp the scum off the bog in their glasses and puffball their cheeks
before the spores fly around the room with the news that the peelers say
It's time to close.

Rosemary Jenkinson

DEFEND THAT

The woman in the white top
with the red lilies and the
black paint strokes
covered all over with sparkling sequins
that sent shards of rainbow
glitter splaying
into the murky
surrounds of the pub, sat reading a menu.

My husband cocked his head
in a curt nod leftwards
glancing to the Barristers
at the next table and said,
"Ask them boys,
 if they could defend that."

Maria McManus

THE ULSTER MUSEUM

The museum
At six
Is big.
It is magic
The walls are very white
They spread very far up
Like airports.
Mostly it's best to go with mummy
Magic is like a world there
It's not like streets and houses
It seems a bit like danger
But not.

Downstairs
Is safe and friendly
The dinosaurs
And fish ponds
It pretends it's not like magic

Upstairs
I take mummy's hand
Some people are not careful
Of the magic
They are silly
I know the danger zones
Where animals jump out corners
And bones are everywhere

My brothers
Go to the 'Living Sea'
I think they are very brave
But I am not that silly
Sometimes I look at it
From the outside
Always five steps away
I do not like monsters in dark places
I am not silly
I go with mummy
We like to see pretty things

Like a big green stone
With white dots
And dresses
On people from years before
That is the magic.

Sometimes but
The magic is strange
They have a dead mummy
In this museum
She is like a ghost to me
I feel sad for her
I don't go near that room
Not even five steps.
My mummy
Is soft and warm
Like bluebells
She smells like mummy

I wonder sometimes about
The little boy
Whose mummy is dead
I think it's very sad
To look at a dead mummy
Also I am afraid of bones

Away from the scary bits
And the nice bits
Is a fairy tale.
Sometimes my mummy
Is like a little person
With big shoes on
One day
We climbed over a rope
Dashed through a big room
With paintings
And found our own gallery

I was afraid
To be found
Sneaking there
Maybe it was wrong

But I like that
The sense that me and
Mummy
Do something bold
This will top the boys
And their silly Living Sea

I think Cinderella
Found her dress here
Always I wanted to visit
Fairyland
This dream comes true
I imagine me in those dresses
With mummy
We would be like princesses.
I am still afraid
Of the magic
I am glad
To come out
Of the forbidden place
Uncaught
Not with the police
I am glad for mummy too
They don't lock little girls up
And mummy has big shoes on

That place
Seemed to disappear
Like magic
I couldn't find it again
I still know the magic
Is there
Inside the walls maybe
Magic sometimes appears
Like a spell
But spells live
Without magic.

Ruth Kennedy

VISIT TO AN ART GALLERY

The tapestry of life hung on the wall,
In one brief hour I saw it all.

Children playing in the street,
A young man in a wheelchair without feet,

Beautiful girls pirouetting in a hall,
Others standing by the red light wall.

Splendid celebrations for Independence Day,
An old man begging with a bowl of clay.

Smiling politicians round a mahogany table,
The world outside a Tower of Babel.

Tranquil countryside with sheep a' grazing,
Tongues of flames, cities blazing.

Graceful swans on a lake afloat,
Powerful battleships on high seas gloat.

A gallery lined with beauty and truth,
I came away as one struck mute.

P. S. Price list available on request.

Catherine O'Sullivan

IF BELFAST HAD...

If Belfast had a mind,
it would be the mind of Mary Beattie,
enquiring, recollecting,
understanding, learning, knowing.

If Belfast had a pair of feet
they would be the feet of Mary Beattie,
acquainted with the paths and byways,
there where it all happens,
covering all ground.

If Belfast had a pair of eyes,
they would be the eyes of Mary Beattie,
noticing, reading, researching,
observing all the life around her,
appreciating all.

If Belfast had a pair of hands,
they would be the hands of Mary Beattie,
making, recording, writing,
creating something new.

If Belfast had a smile,
it would be the smile of Mary Beattie,
open, accepting, welcoming,
full of life's richness and of joy.

Shelley Tracey

A NIGHT TO REMEMBER

This all hallow's eve
moonlight's compassionate streams
touching Belfast's bruised body,
stepping precisely across roof and window
leaves creative footprints in nooks and crannies.

The City Hall's grand statues rejuvenated,
self important people
waltz gracefully around the old mother,
wrapped modestly in tarpaulin
she takes a bath once every fifty years.

One memorial still weeps
annually on that fateful hour,
the crystal dagger
quickly cut the ship's boastful throat.

Stones cry for the old and the new dead,
with not a tissue in sight.
As we rise up together
clinging to the green skinned copper domes,
floating in strange futuristic seas.

Iain C. Webb

THE 'SURVEYOR'

Every day he claims his bench
in a sunny corner of the square.
Clad in old white shabby mac,
a dog-end stuck behind each ear.
Beneath him lie his sole possessions
bulging through two carrier bags,
surveyor of the city's trash cans,
a derelict in recycled rags

There he sits and sips his wine
furtively from an inside pocket,
fantasizing days of glory as he
squints to read a 'bookie's' docket.
Passers- by with sidelong glances
veer to miss his acid tongue
Others cross the street, not seeking
the challenge from this kind of 'bum'

His past, I'm told, was one of comfort,
he owned a big house in the town.
But some say love, and some say business,
one or other brought him down.
Now he wastes his scant existence
drinking wine and planning schemes
but his mind has left for greener pastures
this surveyor of suburban scenes.

Fred McIlmoyle

ON HOPE STREET
(A 'GOODBYE/HELLO')

An apache never says 'goodbye'
And bad cess to thirty years
Of tears of blood, a curse
On both our old bad houses -
(Long runs the fox) so
Hello to our new true brave
Belfast. Braves are good.

Padraic Fiacc

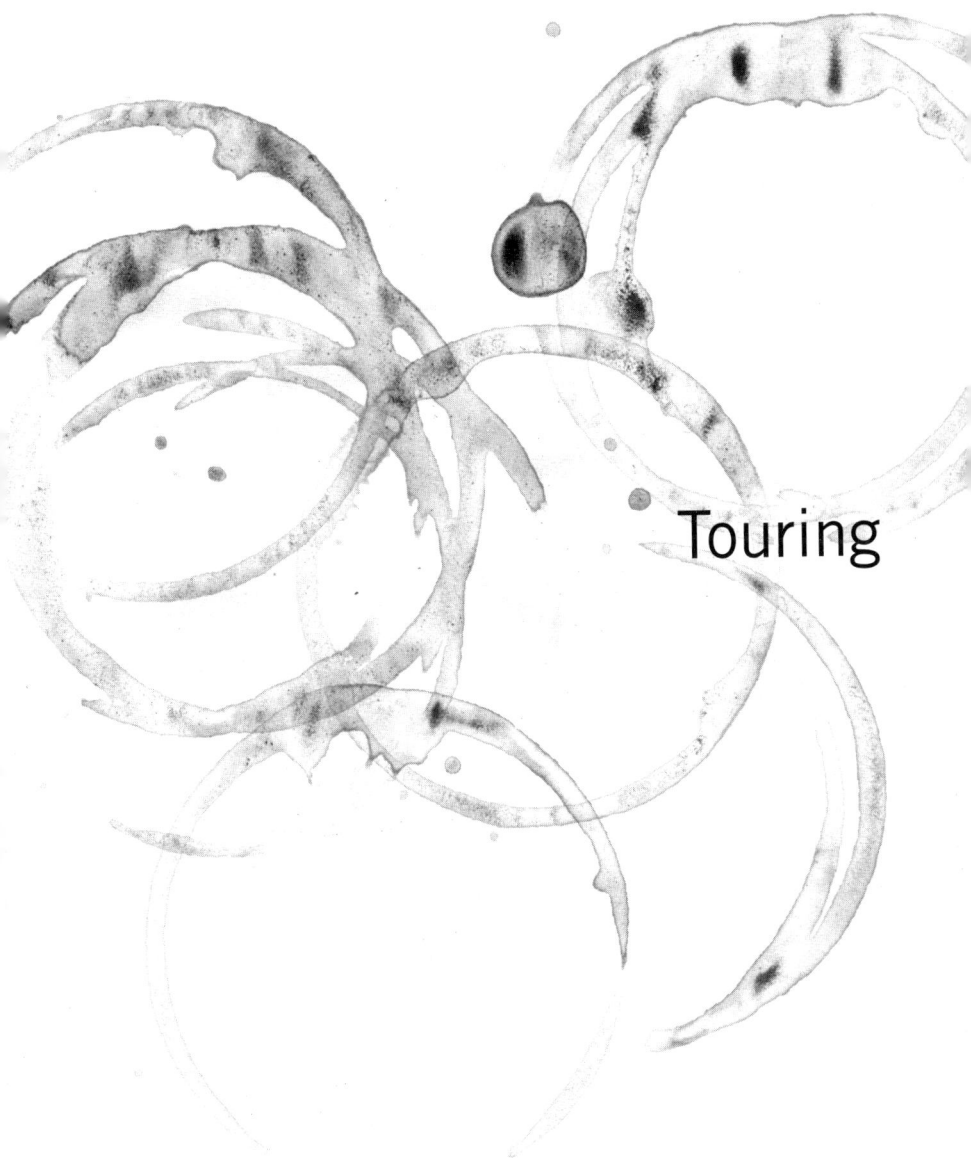

Touring

EMOTIONAL MAP OF GREATER BELFAST

1. ARRIVAL

On this, his first visit, my artist cousin uncurls
a map of Greater Belfast, brings with him
a baggage of colours transported from Manhattan
to his studio in pollution-conscious Portland.
They'd smear blood red across this city's
northern quarter, plumes of smoky-black
igniting in nightfall messaged bottles,
flame-green flak jackets and scowl
of riot shields overlapping in pale washes.

2. THE FIRST TEMPTING

Looking down from Napoleon's Nose I tempt
you to paint a troubled scene. No need
to finger the terraced rows below, we'll
delve in archives at the Linen Hall,
uncover skinny lads in scruffy clothes
posed before a smoking burnt-out van
with hands and scarves to mask their faces. Perhaps
you'd add a cudgel to the smallest nipper's hand
and paint the eyes less harshly; big and watery
and sad. Some sap green and ochre, some soft blue
and yellow to smooth the hard edges of the canvas.

3. THE SECOND TEMPTING

Or might I tempt you tonight from the tallest
rooftop to look north: two bridges straddle
passive Lagan's mauve and blues. The quayside
lights submerge as apparitions, or tiptoe
as angels swayed by the genteel plash of water.
Distant, unpeopled, the city sparkles with clusters
of mellow suns and stars, and arcs of red
and yellow half-moons.
                                                    Above,
the sky is stroked with salmon pink and muted
turquoise releases a genie of dispersing blue
into misty-eyed, chocolate-coated hills.

4. RESOLVE

I offer you these options, assured that either
way you'll make a killing, back in the U.S.A.
I make you think about the spin-offs: posters,
postcards, the tea towel images ....
                                    But
looking down you won't be bound within
these hills and lough and sky. Your eye decodes,
your hand will sift the pieces of an elaborate
jigsaw, etch in black and white the keys
of distant terracing, that slots in perpendiculars,
horizontals as if to form the façade of a Roman
temple. It bleeds its reds to the north of the slate-
grey, curvaceous Lagan.

5. THE JOURNEY

I STORMONT

We balloon down across the city.
I flick through a tourist guide, 'What to See',
veer towards Stormont's Portland stone;
hover over the hum of coaches. Its flock,
unleashed, are clicking Sam or Mary-Bet before
the mile long steep incline.
                            Wanting more
you throw out ballast. We rise above the uniform
rows of lime trees, dip for you to pluck
a bunch of broom, alone, in open fields
beyond the Ice Bowl.

II TULLYCARNET

                            As we soar
above Langholm, Stornoway and Selkirk's high-
rise flats, you put the broom in an endangered
living window, with tieback shimmering
curtains as parenthesis. It burns with an iridescent
flame.

III ANNADALE

Upwards
&
    onwards we view the Lagan from Annadale.
At ground level, road and railings and river
are understated, bland. Only the people
looking downward, introspective, draw
on blue and brown and yellow, as perpendicular
trees and lighting pull the eye to the skyline.
The treetops are delicate as dandelion clocks; a breath
might feather their leaves to the distant liquid
horizon, where sycamores red-tongue the sky.

IV SHAFTSBURY SQUARE

You simplify the colours:
all lines swirl, flood
as black & red rockets.
White tail vapours
intersect in a splash
of vermilion; white
slicks, a fluid screen.

V DIPTYCH

It could be any back street
near the Hammer or Lower
Ormeau. A wall is daubed
with conflicting flags
graffiti. In front you extract
the features of an old man.
Glasses, not quite fitting
corrosive teeth, face
etched with fault-lines.
Wide, hospitable smile
At his feet the pigeons pour
over pockmarks. Several
congeal in a many-
headed mass. One
with wings outstretched
rises into clear
tranquil blue.

A mother, exhausted,
lies full-length
on a bed of straw.
Her baby is pale, delicate
The nurses in Mater & Ulster
uniforms crouch between
the snorting donkeys, look
at the mother's broad
smile. Two windows,
partially open, are rapped
by symmetrical branches.
The tree rocks backwards
and forwards weighted
with symbols of a city's
possibilities, problems.

Ray Givans

North Belfast

VALENTINE STREET

There's a wild eyed moon in Sailortown,
And the faded poster of a clown
By a broken lamppost on Pilot street,
A ruin of glass beneath my feet.

There's a vacant heart in Sailortown,
Darkness pours over the stony ground,
A ship's silhouette slips out to sea,
Vague music drifts over the Lagan quays.

There's no room for romance in Sailortown,
Now they've taken Valentine street down
And the door-step lovers are in exile
With the memory of the fallen miles.

Martin Magee

WATERWORKS

Here in the peaceful early morning
Cavehill and Belfast Castle,
look up Atlantis-like from the still
waters of this large lake.

Here the haughty swan and humble coot
walk ungracefully into the water.
Co-existing, never mixing in the long
forage for food.

Groups of retired men, free at last from
the worries of work.
Stroll around the pond's perimeter,
Debating with enthusiasm the latest
sporting fixture.

On Saturdays gangs of rival football fans,
Their colours on their backs,
chant mindless slogans,
And trade insults on their way
to Solitude.

Here too fresh flowers mark
the spot, where a man was murdered,
While walking home,
One wet winter's afternoon.

Gerry McSorley

COLUMNS

Napoleon's Nose
In February snows.
From lough shores looking up
I recall white jagged tears
Subsiding onto silent trees.
Streets are black in New Lodge and Tiger's Bay
Where souls linger not in cemeteries like they should.
Their resting place is in the columns of the North Belfast News.

Stephen Gharbaoui

SHORE ROAD 2002

In drowsy late summer heat
The Shore Road can overwhelm the senses
Mostly the sense of smell.
The grain bins, the rendering plant
Between the dump and the sewage works
Three breaths bring cloying nausea
Foetid stench of particulate hell
The grass is grey and greasy
And people live there.

Mark Madden

HIGH UP

Where the bluebells grew
So thick
The sky picked up their blue
And the air we breathed
Merged with their scent
High up on Cavehill
With the city below.

Margaret Finlay

South Belfast

JANUARY BOTANIC

The sign in the shop window says
Zanzibar four nine nine or Sri Lanka
five five eight for two sharing. But we two
are here on Botanic, sharing an old umbrella,
our eyes narrowed against wind and sleet.

Then we're in a bar, peeling off our wet coats,
wrapping ourselves in the smoky warmth of music.
Two pints please he shouts to the barman,
And we turn to each other. Shangri-la. Four pounds ten.

Carolyn Thompson

A MOMENT FROM QUEEN'S LIBRARY WINDOW

A mass of softness waddled on swollen ankles and flat feet.
The light, small, fast ball overtakes,
Like a machine intent on culmination.
Different coloured beetles zoom and hum,
The oily blood on which they run,
Is dinner for the tall tanned stationary people,
Who have green hair.

Sandra Johnston

SHARING

I've told you before
will you stop it
stop fighting
you're supposed to share

The North of Ireland cricket club
burned out
the toffs had gone of course
more's the pity.

Was it for spite; for fun;
for revenge;
or a retrieval of territory;
Is it impossible for us to share?

Vivien Paton

THE ORMEAU BRIDGE

On the Ormeau bridge
I stand, where contentious
flames still burn.

Along the Lagan I see
crewmen rowing, faces strained.
Ovens of muscle churning
their oars through
the calm waters
that still flow.

Jim Mawhirk

BOTANICAL GARDENS

In the garden with wind-blown roses washed with rain,
Hoping to come alive again.

The air is claritas
Resin insistent with the scent

Of rain-washed roses washed with rain.

When you have come into this space
It is unclear what bids you out again,

The small hoop of time,
Et nos mutamur in illis,
Day and daylight slight.

Blown into pretty dance,
The petals rubbed smooth,
Washed out with tremulous light.

Cian O'Neill

East Belfast

A SCENE

Sitting in my car at Seapark with requisite chocolate,
a notebook and a view of Cavehill on the other side
of the sea, watching the scenes that present themselves
within the frame of my window screen.

A young woman in flares and shades pushes a child on a swing
who kicks her legs and laughs. For a moment I think it's a scene
from two decades ago of my mother, then not out of her teens,
idling in her one joy. Beside her an older couple

dangle their legs and lick ice creams. A woman in her fifties
Dries off two labradors who scamper and frolic like two
Six year olds. I imagine she married once, quite young,
Had two sons who left home early leaving her and him

To face their differences. Now she's happiest watching
Her two labradors bouncing freely in the waves.
A woman in the car beside me sits in the passenger seat
Dressed darkly and wearing sunglasses while her husband

Runs after his Rottweiler with a poop scoop. He is white-
Haired, wearing Levis and a polo shirt, and eyes up the
Busty teenager strolling through the park. His wife eats
Chocolates and pours herself into her book. Five minutes

Ago a ferry was heaving into view in the east but has now
Gone out of sight through the trees in the west. I think of
My own real fear, of missing the boat, and how everything
Seems to pass without our realising. Soon the toddler on

The swing will be the age her mother is, will someday push
Her own child. Before she knows it she'll be watching her
Husband ogle teenagers while she sits darkly in the passenger
Seat, or perhaps will stroll, as these two do, holding hands
Towards the sun.

Carolyn Jess

96

THE TITANIC RIVET

When I was young my Grandfather spoke
of a ship he built back in his youth.
'Its giant funnels filled Belfast's skies.'
A magnificent liner from Harland and Wolff.

His rope-strung hands held silver steel,
a connection to a former time,
short tapered tail with bulbous head
stamped with the symbols of the White Star Line.

Now when I see pictures of the icy grave
where Titanic lies, flooded with pain,
a porthole opens to another place
and I feel my Grandfather's presence again.

Michael Little

SITTING ON THE BRANIEL BUS

We are very good at sorting,
Categorizing
And filing.

Putting people things and places
Into boxes from which they will never
Escape.

This bus has neatly filed away
Twenty seven people.
The rows   of seats
In tidy   groups
Of twos.

The allocation of seats
Appears to be at random,
No logic or system seems to be in use.
It is only when we move
That the sifting can begin,
And each can be deposited in his
Or her rightful place.

As we pass through each part of the
Town, the bus sieves its occupants
according to religion, class and creed.

The filter is carefully applied.
Here we shake off nationalist
Here loyalist,
This one is for unemployed class,
This for commuting worker.

The bus kneels in homage at each station
Of the cross-town trek
Dispersing with benevolent grace
A home coming pardon for each.

Until it arrives at the terminus
As empty as our labels
To sort, classify and
Condemn.

George Sproule

ASBESTOSIS

Goliath straddles the once proud dock
Now empty but for scraps left
by the Koreans.
Titanic commemorated on celluloid,
No such glory for the scraps of men
Ravaged by the Rip Van Winkle dust
That slept for forty years.

Denis O'Sullivan

ULSTER FARM

In the country places
A kindness and equality prevailed.
The working man was respected
Labouring alongside the farmer
Sharing food at the same table.
Enmity and jealousy were rare
The most pleasing news
Was of people doing well.
Bosses and paid hands were unknown
The land and labour made as one.
This was the County Down way
And my soul delighted in it.

James Snoddy

West Belfast

NOT ONLY IN GOD'S EYE

You can see it from the window of home, bus or train
You can see it from the sky in a high aeroplane
People near and far applaud its mystique
And from wherever they are, can't resist taking a quick peek.
It lies there unaware of all the years of fuss
The place that is a landmark and was a playground for all of us
It may be that there's no sight finer
Than the Great Wall of China (especially from outer space)
But it can't compare
With that icon there
In its own little historical place.
It looks down upon old Belfast Town
Has watched it grow and expand
Many a change it has seen to our dear ancient land,
It observed Belfast grow from a village
To a town and now a city
And many times must have cried out
"For God's sake, have pity!
Don't dig up any more green
To shove in concrete, brick and screen."
It looked down upon the Rock and Springfield dams
Could recall the horse drawn carriages, the dear old trams.
Far below, it could see the local mills
Over the top of mighty 'Goliath' glimpse the Holywood hills,
It can see Castle Buildings
Better known as Stormont to one and all
Fronted by Carson's statue, erect and still tall
It looks upon Cavehill where Napoleon, nose and all
Lies gazing towards heaven, waiting for the call.
Take a ninety degree and it can see
The Mountains of Mourne still sweeping down to the sea.
Closer now lies the cemetery, stretching down to the Falls
A place where we all will go (like it or not), when the man above calls.
Next door is the park where the "Cooler" lay neat,
Making magical waves helped by thousands of feet.

But the council sent boys
With mechanical toys
To fill it in.
A mistake? I think a sin.
It can see Springmartin, Highfield and Ballygomartin
where the men used to spade turf
And just a stone's throw away the good old Murph.
It saw the old church on the Loney, a building once listed
All the demolition man said was, "Christ! I thought we'd missed it."
It was trampled over by many where campers did dwell.
And always within distance of dear old Molly's Well
The children who tiptoed through the buttercups
To crunch one a crime
Blew the fuzz off the dandelions
To find out the time.
They picked the bright bluebells and made long daisy chains
It still hears their giggles
Fond memory retained.
Above its head
They blast off their dynamite and shoot off their lead
Why can't they be like Seamus Heaney
And "dig with the pen" instead?
In the path of the quarryman
With his brutality and force-
Who is it? You ask
Though you may know by now, of course.
Placed there by The Almighty
Sworn never to yield
It is, was, will always be
Our special and only, much loved "Hatchet Field."

Dessie Carabine

THE ROYAL

Victoria sits, tall and regal
Framed by doors of hope
where hushed wards and soft voices
are joined by corridors of mercy
bustling with the sound of racing feet.
Speeding ever faster, to save another soul.

John H. Galbraith

THE STREET SINGER

As midnight fell and time stood still
Through the moonlit shadows of the mill
A lonely figure moved to fill
the night with his sweet song.

With hand curved gently on an ear
His closed eyes hide a secret tear
The song he sang for all to hear
was Ave Maria.

Down the dim lit street past the gable wall
His echoed voice my thoughts recall
Kind neighbours gathered in their hall
To hear his song of love.

But now as morning light breaks through
More visions slowly fade from view
The streets the houses old friendships too
Like yesterday have gone adieu.

Vincent Dargan

FALLS PARK

When your only friend is the Falls Park
solitary pathways
tarmac rivers
pitched slopes.

On benches under elderly pines, older people
think themselves children
making chains with bygone daisies
tickling fading buttercup chins
presenting mammy with drooping wet-the-beds
in handed down sloppy-jo's
tansad races going nowhere
transistors searching for Athlone,
waiting for the slider woman.

The crowds have all got cars now,
and Euro passports to the sun.
On these few acres
the questions are yours now.

Who?
Built that basalt cemetery wall
Who?
Is the tearaway on the quad
Passing
No alcohol signs
and scores of teenage juice-merchants
Who
urinate on pines
with semi-diluted alcohol.
Progress with a capital P.

What ghost sat on this old seat?

Nature is in the ageing face here
hectic hustle
bubbling Falls
forgiven, forsaken.

It is some seventh day
sport is being played,
relax in these Falls meadows
and await your slider woman.

Tony Fitzpatrick

THE SPLENDOURS OF SOLITUDE

I am Ben Madigan king of twelve centuries
Abdicated now ascended by nature.
Standing proud as tall as is tall
I have become known to many,
And through my misty exhale you greet me
As one of the many.
With feet entangled rooted in bracken briar
Comb your toes through thorny locks
Once fair, now aged, matted in gale or on storm.
Your fingers stroke my brow until the dew drop of spring runs freely
Freely of cupped palm to the waiting thirst of Foxglove,
Whereupon this life is assured, but a blink of an eye sends poison.
Down through golden buttercup meadows
To bog land marshy tongue.
The gurgle of whispers swirl over rocky, moulding teeth,
That chatter and chirp with bird song.
Angels dance from rolling cloud
My bearded heaven, a haven of holy wonder.
I possess the sun on your smiling face
In return you are radiant in warmth.
Come twilight and the nightingale lullaby,
A blood red sky drifts o'er a sea of stars,
Whereupon tiring sun finds my shadow.
Sailing on the lower Lough the moon pulls the waves,
Ever closer and closer to lava flow lights
That flow in my vale.
My aging eyes look forth
We meet under a sea of tranquillity,
Mirrored on tide the shape of importance.
I am Ben Madigan king of twelve centuries
In my arms a queen of solace of destiny
And unequalled importance.
My old and wise ways held her hand.

Matt Garrett

Belfast Walks

WALKING AT STORMONT

There is a point along the path where the clamorous rush of traffic
rolls like the ocean, its inexorable swell engulfing the outside world.
I dream the surrounding streets submerged, waves lapping at the gates,
access to the highground of the chieftains by coracle only.
Bearing the sound in mind, the sea in my blood,
I shun the muscle-pulling stretch towards Carson,
rising without sense of incline until Stormont shocks into sight,
pale posts unyielding through gauzy cherry-blossom,
the windows glinting with entrapment, a reminder of hard labour.
I turn my back, content to stay strayed off the beaten track.

Here is nature's seat of government: an assembly of blackbirds
voting with their feet, scuffling through bracken in heated debate
as wood-pigeons' wings ripple through the canopy, applauding
the eloquent oration of birdsong, voicing all that needs said.
Finches dismember larch cones, their squabble unsettling
dignified trunks of birch peeling imperiously on the forest floor.
Then a wilderness of ferns, their fronds warm to the touch,
unfurl above the peaty earth with quiet grace
while the trees crowd in, pungent foliage heady with solidarity,
swallowing my footfall in their dampening bark.

Below a parliament of crows I find awareness,
accepting such diverse opinion in the wood,
these party boundaries, splinter groups,
for once entirely understood.

Lindsay Hodges

EVENING VISIT TO A GRAVEYARD

Evening falls, and soon the moon will rise to chart its silver wake
While I, my heart in shreds, dread the thought,
that I will perish one day,
and wonder who will cherish my memory?
Then tears fall and I hear the distant call of a bird
and from its sweetness
I ask the Lord to hear my prayer,
"If to dust I must return,
Wrap me in birdsong."

Noreen Campbell

CABIN FEVER

All day long the babies prowled the flat,
demented gerbils looking for something to shred.
Sometimes it was bearable: a small tight ship
surfing on waves of winter, the wind and rain
kept at bay by the babies' soft breath furring
the glass, fat hands making snail trails, lop-sided moons
blotting out the freezing street below.
But mostly they girned and she gazed at the wet black branches,
like prison bars, only moving, casually
slicing her window into twitchy segments
spiked with rain like bits of broken glass
stuck on a wall to stop you getting over.
They slept, she smoked, she couldn't stop, the flat
was starved of oxygen by the time they crashed
into wakefulness, both at once, with a single scream.
She bundled them out to the park but still it felt
like indoors: overflowing rubbish bins,
cramped threadbare grass, the swings pushed over the top
so many times, they were tangled out of reach,
flurries of sleet scudding down from a sour sky
pale and congealed, like left-over scrambled egg.
Next time they slept she left them with a neighbour,
and put herself on a bus going anywhere.

The terminus was half way to the skyline.
Pine trees, brambles, gorse already gold.
She scrambled the last bit and stood amazed:
acres and acres of rough grass, soft moss, bog,
white whisps on stems that looked like cotton wool
or butterflies, if you half closed your eyes,
and small brown birds spurting out of the heather, rising
and falling, tseep tseep, a mocking flurry of wings,
and up there some kind of hawk wheeling and gliding
in a luminous sky with no branches, poles or wires.
She lay on the dry - enough heather and gazed and gazed,
with the fine rain misting her hair, the juice of rainbows
seeping into her tired mind, cradling her
in a long slow ecstasy poised between soaring and sleep.

She thought of her neighbour frantic, the babies awake.
She pulled off one of her rings and left it wedged
under a rock, as if the tiny circle
of light would spin in the shadows in her head
in the restless short spring nights and carry it all
to her crowded bedside: the whole vast sweep of the hill,
sinuous, endless, the ripple of wind on grass.
I'll be back, she said to the white butterflies, to herself,
I'll be back soon, wait for me, beginning the trudge
down to where the stale air, mud-fogged windows
of the last bus waited, grumbling, to carry her home.

Janet Shepperson

RANDOM THOUGHTS

The trouble with me is I'm not really old.
Seventy last birthday, Alzheimer's' "On-hold"

I take myself a walk and I see what I see.
No silver spumed tides, broken shored on Tralee
Only stone paved paths. Tarmac roads unexplored.
Square footed gardens where distant horizons I'd known.

Contented now, the mad race has been run.
Hard earned this place in winter's sun.
So I pretend to be better than really I was.
Unseeding wild schemes afore a world so fettered.
Endlessly exaggerate my minor successes.
Rave about girls in flower-print dresses
For the praise and applause of those unaware
Of my little flaws.

And should my thoughts turn towards
A rollicking good fight,
That bloody Social Worker still visits
– every – Friday – night!

Axel R McMasters

Meeting Points

CLEARING THE SOCK DRAWER

In here   are forty-seven
pairs of   socks enjoying
monogamous   relationships;

And   eleven   who   have   recently   been
Divorced,
With one partner living elsewhere -
In illicit liaison with shirts, boxers or the
Fluff from the tumble dryer.

The remaining partner has little hope of
Being paired off with another of a different shade.
Mixed marriages don't work in here,
They're not considered socially acceptable.

A few are too festive for their own good.
Courtesy of a colour blind
Outofhermind
Muchtookind aunt
They lurk at the back awaiting a
Visit.

For   some,
Their   time
Has   come,

Showing the ravages of unfit footwear
They are now more hole than sock,
And I have to be in dire need of their company
Before I will reacquaint them with my shoes.

And   thus,
They   must
Leg   it.

George Sproule

COINCIDENCE?

What if I hadn't gone to Belfast that day,
That summer afternoon in '62?
What if I'd turned and walked the other way
In Fountain Street, and not bumped into you?
Tongue-tied, confused, I felt my senses soar
And I could hardly still my beating heart;
For we had parted thirteen months before
And all that time we had remained apart.
So there we were, as if those months had passed
As but a day, our love reborn again
As strong as ever; strong enough to last
Through forty years of friendship, joy and pain.
I look at daughter Ros and baby Kate,
Would they be here if you or I'd been late?

John Mercer

SOMEONE ELSE'S STORY

is knit into my skin.
I have tried to undo the stitches
but my face will always place me

like a fisherman's geansai
where each knit, purl and loop
forms the mark of a village

they have rendered their pattern on me
and even in death they will have me.

Deirdre Cartmill

Unravelled. Like the Fisherman's rib I knitted for you.
Mother thought it too baggy, for a slight female.
Transformed it into a tightly woven Aran.
I cried as she made me try it on.
She wasn't to know that it wasn't out of gratitude.

I'd made it big deliberately for someone bigger than I
Would ever be. To keep you warm in summers that were
More like winters to you then. I naively imagined that
What I wanted to tell you, would communicate by osmosis
Through every thread. I made it baby blue, to match the eyes
Of the traveller.

Like stripes of abstract art, I do not understand why I could never
Wear it when you did come home.

Time. Time would pass, though I never saw it. Soon years would pass
Without me seeing you. Sitting at the computer, in the corner. Wearing
An old green, holey, cardigan that made you look older than you were
And I felt ripped. Holding back the choke that threatened to asphyxiate me.

With my heart you got the finished article. You weren't to know how
Many times the pattern had changed. But it's amazing what a girl can
Do when she puts her mind to it.

A running stitch that kept popping up unexpectedly. A dark stranger, always.

Jacqui McMenamin

RESEARCH

I just do. Like you, I mean.
Your navy blue eyes,
Your tendency to blush.
The way I could eat every soft, ample, part of you.
When you look in my direction,
I challenge you to look away.
The big words you say beautifully
Which I fire back at you like
Love tipped arrows.

Could I be your objective and
Be the data only you can analyse
I want to tell you my theories and
Have you prove yours.
We could find the median between us,
And explore new areas of investigation.
What would you say the ratio is.

Jaqui McMenamin

AMPHIBIAN

Swimming to me
through the channels
of this life
Like an eel or some
redundant sea creature
Perch on my back
my hand stroking tail fins and dorsel.
For you I'd slash my neck,
your word is my raft
Dive into my depths
I'll sate your dry land
and rise and fall, glistening as if
with sweat
in a cobalt sea and sky.
Navigator - there is nothing hidden now
our bodies lithe, weightless
cleansed in the sea of
knowingness-
Drowning in love.

Maria Doyle

PLUM

Out of the blue
This late summer eve
Wild, ripe fruit
Has fallen like manna
Voluptuously
On the soft
Yielding ground
Of my bed
Making the room orchard
Vapours of
Spiced melon
Sparkling peach
A hint of pepper
Vanilla,
Trace of musk
Swirls in a
Swooning head
And I
Lone harvester
Climbing the
Apples and pears

Royce Harper

A SHELTERED DWELLING IN BELFAST

My first born
Tonight experienced pain.
Her friend
I think he loves her
Disclosed the truth
About people
Blinded by mistrust,
History
And ignorance
She says.
He says
That it does not matter to him.
She finds it hard to comprehend
How his parents can make judgments
Hate people they do not know.

David Smylie

the right thing
the wrong video

"It's the wrong video", I told the bloke
this wedding is plush
the bride blushing
White silk graces perfect bodies
and no one has a hair out of place or
puts a foot wrong.

My video can't be like that
cos my wedding wasn't like that.

Kids screamed at the back
and the bulge
bulged

Still at least he's doin
the right thing
Aunt Edna had said to the camera
full on bold as you like
The right thing

His mates were too drunk or stoned to stand

"The woman in this video"
I said
looks like a princess

there were no princesses at my wedding
They fled in terror as they turned the corner to face head on
the portacabined registry office.

Still at least he's doin'
The Right Thing
said his mum's sister
arms wrapped in consolation
around his mother
        her sister
        my mother in law

There are no such moments in this video
I told the bloke

This Dallas
not Chaos
This is chauffeur driven
not dodgey Capri
broken down on the hard shoulder.

Special Occasions
Videos
recorded from only £30
that's
what
the ad had said
and my Ronny knows a bargain when he sees one,
so he took the £30 special offer
and the piss.

"I wonder who's got yours then?"
the bloke said

the baby turned in my belly
at the thought of it.

"I dunno." I said.
"But I hope it's not the Police."

Jani X

LITTLE SHAREEM

BBC TV Afghanistan.

Better three thousand dead
and not one vengeful finger raised
to add you to that number.

Above the veil
your mother's eyes lament.
I am invaded by the pain.

Two years wise,
weight two bags of sugar;
there are no crumbs for you,
no blanket but the snow.

Pat Taylor

Resource Information

New Belfast
Community Arts Initiative

Poetry in Motion is one of several projects from the New Belfast Community Arts Initiative.

New Belfast Community Arts Initiative consists of key umbrella groups from across Belfast: providing the maximum possible inclusiveness, capacity building and training towards self- sustainability.

We work in the most socially and economically deprived areas of Belfast, providing innovative, cross -community projects which facilitate personal and community self - empowerment and transformation through new ways of being, seeing and doing.

By focusing on our shared humanity and common needs and aspirations, we challenge the artificially contrived cultural, social and other barriers which keep people apart.
In this way, we seek to contribute to a better future for all our citizens.

The consortium includes:

Arts for All	02890 875 000
Community Arts Forum	02890 242 910
Cultúrlann McAdam Ó Fiaich	02890 964 186
Greater East Belfast Community Arts Network	02890 451 512
Northern Ireland Council for Ethnic Minorities	02890 238 645
North Belfast Communities in Action	02890 740 693
Shankill Community Arts Network	02890 223 445
South Belfast Cultural Society	02890 321 766
Open Arts	02890 312 515
Upper Springfield Youth Network	02890 805 555

New Belfast Community Arts Initiative
Unit 4, Clanmil Arts & Business Centre
Bridge Street, Belfast
BT1 1LU

T: 02890 923493 F: 02890 924545
E: info@newbelfastarts.org
W: www.newbelfastarts.org

©WN

Creative Writers' Network
c/o Jo Egan
15 Church Street, Belfast
BT1 1FF
Tel: 02890 312 361

The Creative Writers' Network is a network of individual writers and writers groups which facilitate the comprehensive development of creative writing in Northern Ireland.

CWN is a central information point, which provides advice, information and support for writers and potential writers. It provides year round activities including master classes, workshops, training, events and performances. It publishes a quarterly bulletin and has also published an anthology of poetry and short stories called "Alchemy."

CWN annually hosts the prestigious Brian Moore Short Story Awards.

National Organisations

Queen's English Society
School of English
Queen's University
Belfast
BT7 1NN
www.qub.ac.uk
Tel: 02890 335 103
The Queen's University English Society organises a wide range of readings, lectures and social events during the academic year. The Society is supported by the Arts Council of Northern Ireland, which enables it to bring an exciting number of writers and academics to Belfast each year.

Children's Express
3 Rosemary Street
Belfast
BT1 1QA
belfastenquiries@fsmail.net
www.childrens-express.org
Tel: 02890 232 --032
Fax: 02890 438 828
Children's Express is a programme of learning through journalism for eight to 18 year olds.

Verbal Arts Centre
Stable Lane
Bishop Street Within
Derry BT48 6PU
T: 02871 266 946
F: 02871 263 638
The Verbal Arts Centre aspires to bring together the spoken and written word and to unite listening and reading with speaking and writing. It regards the oral tradition as an important seedbed for written literature, as well as for conveying the musicality of language and a sense of community and identity. The Centre stresses the creative and imaginative potential of language and has consistently promoted the right of every person to be able to articulate his or her feelings, dreams, aspirations or fears.

The Poetry Society
22 Betterton Street
Covent Garden
London WC2H 9BU Map
Tel: 0171 420 9880
E: info@poetrysociety.org.uk
Publishes 'Poetry Review' and 'Poetry News'. Operates the Poetry Place café and performance venue in Covent Garden, London. Organises National Poetry Day and the annual National Poetry Competition.

Irish National Poetry Organisation
Upper Yard, Dublin Castle
Dublin 2 Ireland.
Tel: +353 (0)1 6714632
Fax: +353 (0)1 6714634
Email: poetry@iol.ie
A 32 county body supported by The Arts Council of Ireland and The Arts Council of Northern Ireland. Acts as the central contact for anything to do with poetry in Ireland. Core activities are: publications, readings, education and a resource centre. Also curates the Austin Clarke Library, the John Jordan Library and a contemporary poetry Library.

Poetry Libraries

Central Library
Royal Avenue
Belfast BT1
Tel: 02890 509 150
A central resource for Belfast, the library has a large collection of poetry and arts magazines as well as access to the internet.

Bangor Library
c/o Stephen Hanson, Branch Librarian
80 Hamilton Road
Bangor BT20 4LH
Tel: 02891 270 591
Fax: 02891 462744
E:bangorlib@hotmail.com
www.seelb.org.uk
The only recognised poetry place in Northern Ireland with accreditation from the Poetry Society. The library features a collection of poetry, mainly post - 1950s, focusing on local writers, with a broader range of national and international poets. There are regular evenings of readings, talks and workshops with a poetry noticeboard. The library also holds a collection of poetry related magazines and is willing to accept donations from local writers.

Linen Hall Library
17 Donegal Square North
Belfast BT1 5GB
Tel: 02890 321 707
E: info@linenhall.com
Based in Belfast city centre since its foundation in 1788, the Linen Hall Library is the city's oldest library, the last subscribing library in Ireland, and houses one of the most renowned collections of Irish material in the world. The library offers a programme of events and readings across the disciplines of literature and art, including reading groups on the last Thursday of each month, workshops and talks from contemporary poets.

Irish Writers' Centre
19 Parnell Square
Dublin 1
Tel: +353 (0) 1 8713102
E: info@writerscentre.ie
Housed in three stories of a building in 19 Parnell Square, Dublin 1, the Irish Writers' Centre was established to promote and assist in the development of contemporary Irish writing. It acts as an umbrella body for four constituent organisations: The Irish Children's Book Trust, The

Irish Translators' Association, The Irish Writers' Union, and the Irish Playwright's and Screenwriter's Guild.

The Northern Poetry Library
The Willows, Morpeth
Northumberland NE61 1TA
Tel: 01670 512385
E:amenities@northumberland.gov.uk
Membership (free) for residents of Cleveland, Cumbria, Durham, Northumberland, and Tyne and Wear. Non-residents can become associate members.

The Saison Poetry Library
Level 5, Royal Festival Hall
London SE1 8XX
T: 020 7921 0943/0664
F:020 7921 0939
Email - info@poetrylibrary.org.uk
A comprehensive collection of English language poetry and poetry in translation, plus audio and video facilities, and a large stock of poetry magazines. Also carries up-to-date information on poetry competitions, workshops and specialist bookshops. Membership is free.

Scottish Poetry Library
5 Crichton's Close
Canongate
Edinburgh EH8 8DT
Features online access to the INSPIRE catalogue, and downloadable samples from the Jewel Box project. Home of the European Poetry Information Centre.
T: 0131 557 2876 F: 0131 557 8393
E: inquiries@spl.org.uk
Personal membership 10 UK pounds per annum.

Poems in the Waiting Room
PO Box 488
Kew, Richmond TW9 4SW
E: leelda@globalnet.co.uk
The service provides free poetry leaflets for patients to read while waiting to see their doctor. Submissions of suitable poems for publication would be welcome as well as suggestions of health centres who might like to receive the complimentary service. Guidelines and invitation leaflets available from Michael Lee.

The National Poetry Foundation (UK)
27 Mill Road Fareham
Hants PO16 0TH
T: 01329 822218

Greater Belfast multi - arts (including literary) Festivals

Castlereagh Verbal Arts Festival	1 week in February
Between the Lines	10 days in March/April
Cathedral Quarter Arts Festival	First 10 days in May
Sailortown Festival	June
Greater Shankill Festival	Mid June for 3 weeks
John Hewitt Summer School	Mid July
Féile an Phobail/ West Belfast Festival	August
Ardoyne Fleadh	August
Short Strand Community Festival	August
McCracken School	Late Summer
Aspects Festival	September
The Open House	October
Belfast Festival at Queen's	October/November

Ardoyne Fleadh
43, Herbert Street
Belfast BT14 7FE
Tel: 02890 751 056 Fax: 02890 751 055
E: info@cinni.org

Aspects, a Celebration of Irish Writing
c/o Gail Prentice, The Arts Officer
North Down Borough Council
Tower House
34, Quay Street
Bangor BT20 5ED
Tel: 02891 278 032 Fax: 02891 467 744
E: arts.officer@northdown.gov.uk

The Belfast Festival at Queen's
c/o Stella Hall
Festival House
25 College Gardens
Belfast BT9 6BS.
Tel: 02890 667 687 Fax: 02890 663 733
W: www.belfastfestival.com

Between The Lines Festival
The Crescent Arts Centre
2-4 University Road
Belfast BT7 1NH.
Tel. 02890 242 339 Fax: 02890 246 748.
E: info@crescentsarts.org

Castlereagh Verbal Arts Festival
c/o Kim Cobain, Arts Officer
Castlereagh Borough Council
Civic Centre
Bradford Court
Belfast BT8 6RB
Tel: 02890 494 500 Fax: 02890 494 555

Cathedral Quarter Arts Festival
c/o Sean Kelly
20 North St. Arcade
Belfast BT1 1PB
Tel: 02890 232 403 Fax: 02890 319 884
cqaf@hotmail.com
www.cqaf.com

Féile an Phobail
c/o Carol Jackson
Teách na Féile
473 Falls Road
Belfast BT12 6DD
Tel: 02890 313 440 Fax: 02890 319 150
W: www.feilebelfast.com

Greater Shankill Festival
c/o Pheme Brown
250a, Shankill Road
Belfast BT13 2BL
Tel: 02890 311 333 E: feebro@hotmail.com

John Hewitt International Summer School
c/o The Administrator
7 Botanic Avenue
Belfast BT7 1JG,
Tel. 02890 793 008
E: info@johnhewitt.org
www.johnhewitt.org

McCracken Summer School
c/o Mairtin Campbell
174 Trust
Duncairn Complex
Duncairn Avenue
Belfast BT14 6BP
Tel: 02890 749 688

The Open House
c/o Kieran Gilmore
The John Hewitt Pub
Donegal Street
Belfast BT1
Tel: 02891 454754

Sailortown Festival
c/o Paul McLaughlin
65, Dock Street
Belfast BT1
Tel: 02890 751 094

Short Strand Community Festival
26a, Beechfield Street
Short Strand Community Centre
Belfast BT5 4EQ
Tel: 02890 501 7000

Writing Classes

There are classes in creative writing (including poetry) every day of the working week in Belfast. This is a snapshot of the level of interest just in poetry from September, 2002 for courses that last up to 28 weeks - we include this as a touchstone to the interest in poetry, as well as the varied interests of creative writing.

Monday 10 - 12	BIFHE Parkmore, Ormeau Road
Monday 10 - 12	Conway Education Centre, Conway Mill
Tuesday 10 - 12	Woodstock Library
Wednesday 10 - 12	Falls Library
Wednesday 10.30 - 1	Newtownabbey Senior Citizens' Forum
Wednesday 6.30 - 8.30	BIFHE Parkmore, Ormeau Road
Thursday 10 - 12	Shalom House, Cliftonville Road
Thursday 7 - 9.30	Ards Arts Centre, Newtownards
Friday 11 - 1	Shalom House, Cliftonville Road
Friday 10 - 12	Whiterock, Whiterock Road

There will be new classes for other terms, in other years. These fee-paying classes exist because of the level of interest. There are other classes that have as great an interest such as in the short story, the novel, writing stories for children and screenwriting.

For complete and updated details of what courses are currently available, contact your local adult education providers:

**Belfast Institute of
Further and Higher Education**
Information Services
Park House
87 -91 Great Victoria Street
Belfast BT2 7AG
Tel: 02890 265 265
www.belfastinstitute.ac.uk
Contact: Jill Parton 02890 234 055
jparton@belfastinstitute.ac.uk

Workers' Educational Association
1-3 Fitzwilliam Street
Belfast BT9 6AW
Tel: 02890 329 718
www.wea-ni.com
Contact: Julieanne McCormick
julieanne.mccormick@wea-ni.com

For accredited courses, contact the following further education sources:

NI Open College Network
Accredited Creative Writing
BIFHE College Square East
Tel: 02890 234 055

The Open University
Tel: 02890 245 025

**Queen's University
Institute of Continuing Education**
Tel: 02890 245 133

**Queen's University MA Diploma English
(Creative Writing)**
Queen's University Belfast
English Department
Tel: 02890 245 133

**University of Ulster
Department of Continuing Education**
Tel: 02890 365 131 (Jordanstown Campus)

*For information and guidance
on all the above educational choices contact:*

Educational Guidance Service for Adults
4th Floor, 40 Linenhall Street
Belfast BT2 8BA
Tel: 02890 244 274

Writers' Groups & Libraries: North

Hammer Writers
Denis and Rene Craig,
Ballysillan and Ardoyne
Community Group
Benview Park
Belfast BT14
Tel: 02890 875 134
E: catherine.greig@ntlworld.com
Last Tuesday of each month

Newtownabbey Writers
Jim Johnston
9 Kings Parade
Newtownabbey BT37 0DL
Tel: 02890 853 159
First Wednesday of each month
7pm - 10pm
Venue Changes
jimzilla@aladdinscave.net

Giros Poetry Collective
1-5 Donegall Lane
Belfast BT1 2LZ
E: bycg@dial.pipex.com
Tel: 02890 244 640
Fax: 02890 315 629

Ardoyne Library
446 - 450 Crumlin Road
Tel: 02890 509 202

Chichester Library
Salisbury Avenue
Tel: 02890 509 210

Ligoniel Library
53 -55 Ligoniel Road
Tel: 02890 509 221

Oldpark Road Library
46 Oldpark Road
Tel: 02890 509 226

Skegoneill Library
Skegoniell Avenue
Tel: 02890 509 244

Writers' Groups & Libraries: South

**Crescent Arts
Centre Writers' Workshop**
Mairtin Crawford,
Crescent Arts Centre
2-4 University Road
Belfast BT17 1PA
Tel: 02890 242 338
E: martin-crawford@lineone.net
Meets on Thursday evenings at
7.30 - 9.30

**Queen's University
of Belfast Writers**
Sinead Morrisey, School of
English
University Road, Queen's
University
Belfast BT7 1NA
Tel: 028 90 273 678
W: www.qub.ac.uk
Peter Froggatt Centre
Wednesdays at 4-6 pm

Writers' Club
Shirley Bork
Lagan Valley Island
The Island Arts Centre
Lisburn BT27 4RL
Tel: 02892 509 509
Meets on Fridays 2 -4

Finaghy Library
13 Finaghy Road South
Tel: 02890 509 214
Lisburn Road Library
440 Library Road
Tel: 02890 509 223

Ormeau Road Library
247 Ormeau Road
Tel: 02890 509 228

Sandy Row Library
127 Sandy Row
Tel: 02890 509 230

Writers' Groups & Libraries: East

Ards Writers
Ruth Thompson
31 Wanstead Park
Dundonald, Co. Down
BT16 2EX
Tel: 02890 481 221

Belfast Burns Club Association
Ann Allen
32 Cumberland Park
Dundonald
Belfast
BT16 0AZ
Tel: 02890 489 342

Creative Writing Class
Jo Knock
Greenway Women's Centre
19 Greenway
Belfast BT6 0DT
Tel: 02890 799 912
E: greenwaywomen@cinni.org
Meets on Tuesdays 1 - 3pm

Double Helix
Myra Vennard
4 Sandymount Court
Bangor BT20 4UE
Tel: 02891 459 592

Harland and Wolff Burns Club
2 Harland Park
Belfast
BT4 1HZ

Holywood Writers
The Holywood Centre
Val McAvoy
Tel: 02891 276 700

Muse Writers
Thelma Sheil
88 Lyle Road
Bangor BT20 5LX
Tel: 02891 463 674
Not Regular

Sister Scribes
Betty McIlroy
Age Concern
24, Hamilton Road
Bangor BT20
Tel: 02891 451 551
Meets Mondays 10.30 - 12.30
All-women writers and
performance group.

**Word of Mouth Poetry
Collective**
Ruth Carr
159 Lower Braniel Road
Belfast BT5 7NN
Tel: 02890 795 464
Women only. By invitation only.

Ballyhackamore Library
1 - 4 Eastleigh Drive
Tel: 02890 509 204

Ballymacarrett Library
19 - 35 Templemore Avenue
Tel: 02890 509 207

Cairnmartin Library
Mount Gilbert Community
School
Ballygomartin Road
Tel: 02890 509 241

Holywood Arches Library
4- 12 Holywood Road
Tel: 02890 509 216

Whitewell Library
41 -83 Serpentine Road
Newtownabbey
Tel: 02890 509 242

Woodstock Library
358 Woodstock Road
Tel: 02890 509 239

Writers' Groups & Libraries: West

Black Mountain Writers
Dolores Craig
54 Gransha Park
Belfast BT11 8AU
Tel: 02890 203 190

Divis Writers
Divis Community Centre
9b Ardmoulin Place
Belfast BT12 4RT
Tel: 02890 242 551
Fax: 02890 313 924

Roddy McCorley Writers
Jim McCabe + Liam Donnelly
Roddy McCorley Social Club
Moyard House, Glen Road
Belfast BT11 8BT
Tel: 02890 228 148
Wednesday 7.30 - 9.30 pm

Stadium Writers
Bernard Langford
Fernhil House
Glencairn Road
Belfast BT12 8HQ
Tel: 02890 715 599

Andersonstown Library
Slievegallion Drive
Tel: 02890 509 200

Falls Road Library
49 Falls Road
Tel: 02890 509 212

Shankill Road Library
298-300 Shankill Road
Tel: 02890 509232

Suffolk Library
Stewartstown Road
Tel: 02890 509 234

Whiterock Library
10 Whiterock Road
Tel: 02890 509 236

Useful websites for poetry

An tUltach
www.cnag.ie/ultach.htm

Arts Council of Northern Ireland
www.artscouncil-ni.org

Belfast City Council arts directory
www.belfastcity.gov.uk/arts
/artsdatabase

British Council
www.britishcouncil.org/arts
/literature

Community Arts Forum
www.caf.ie

Glossary of Poetic Terms
www.library.utoronto.ca/utel
/rp/poetterm.html

Irish Poetry Ulster Scots
www.geocities.com/briaind
/nyuck2.htm

Irish Writers Centre
www.writerscentre.ie

Irish Writers Online
www.irishwriters-online.com

Live Literature
www.liveliterature.net

Poetry Ireland
www.poetryireland.ie

Poetry for Kids
www.poetry4kids.com
/poems.html

The Poetry Kit
www.poetrykit.org/Ireland

Poetry Society
www.poetrysoc.com

Salmon Poetry Press
www.salmonpoetry.com

trace online writing community
www.trace.ntu.ac.uk

The Arcadia Sessions by Mark Madden

Since 1997, Arcadia Coffeehouse in North St. Arcade has been the home of the North's only regular open mic session. I had recently returned from Vancouver, where I had been helping organise events, and performing at many more. When I realised there were no performance poetry venues in Belfast, I felt compelled to start one. This was a strong impetus toward opening the cafe.

We have no particular genre or age group at the sessions; some poems are meditative, some hilarious. We don't use lists, timers or points. You don't have to give your name. There is a core group of regulars who between them give the readings their unique flavour, many of whom gig in other venues, and organise events themselves. The atmosphere is informal and occasionally bawdy. We have spawned a new organisation called Critical Mass Performance Poets, so local poets can work together to reach a wider audience.

We always welcome new poets, and are happy to liaise with others to help create new venues or events. Currently the readings take place on the first Friday of each month at the coffeehouse, and we run other cultural events throughout the month. We can be contacted on 02890 330 370, or by e-mail at: baphie@hotmail.com

Venues often used for poetry readings

For a further listing check out "Where do you get hold of Them'ns" from the Community Arts Forum.

Arcadia Café
c/o Mark Madden
North Street Arcade
Belfast BT1 1PA
Tel: 02890 330 370
E: baphie@hotmail.com

The Atrium
Clanmil House
c/o Jim Pow
Northern Whig House
Waring Street
Belfast BT1 1LU
Tel: 02890 876 000
E: jim.pow@clanmil.org.uk

Bookfinders Café
Mary Denvir
46 University Road
Belfast BT7 1NJ
Tel: 02890 328 269

Crescent Arts Centre
2 -4 University Road
Belfast BT7 1NH
Tel:02890 242 338 Fax:
02890 246 748
E: info@crescentarts.org

Cultúrlann McAdam Ó Fiaich
216 Bóthar na bhFál,
Belfast BT12 6AH
T: 02890 964 180
E: eimear@irelandclick.com

First Step Drop in Centre
York Road, Belfast
BT15
Tel: 02890 744 040

Grace and Groove Café
44 Belmont Road
Belfast BT4 2AN
Tel: 02890 655 377

The John Hewitt Pub
51 Donegall Street
Belfast BT1 2FH
Tel: 02890 233 768

Linen Hall Library
17 Donegal Square North
Belfast BT1 15GB

Tel: 02890 321 707
Fax: 02890 438 586

Lagan Look Out
1 Donegall Quay
Belfast BT1 3EA
Tel: 02890 315 444

Lyric Theatre
55, Ridgeway Street
Belfast BT9
Tel: 02890 669 660
W: www.lyrictheatre.co.uk

The Menagerie Bar
130 University Street
Belfast BT7 1HH
Tel: 02890 235 678

Postscript Café
537 Antrim Road
Belfast
BT15 5GP
Tel: 02890 772 880

174 Trust
Duncairn Avenue
Belfast BT14 6BP

HU- The Honest Ulsterman by Ruth Carr

This poetry magazine, founded by the late James Simmons in 1968, has published the work of established and new writers alongside one another, as well as carrying reviews and literary essays on a wide range of authors by its regular contributor "Jude the Obscure". The magazine has gone through many editors since James Simmons - Michael Foley, Frank Ormsby, Robert Johnstone, Ruth Hooley (Carr), Tom Clyde and Irish language editor, Frankie Sewell, as well as guest editors such as Sam Burnside and Ann McKay. Despite the irregularity of its appearances at times, HU (as it has come to be known)has successfully showcased the work of many poets in pamphlet form, including that of Medbh McGuckian, Ian Duhig, Kerry Hardy, Cathal O'Searcaigh and Joan Newmann. However, it has not managed to live up to its founder's aspirations, as expressed in the original subtitle to this sixties magazine - The Honest Ulsterman, a Handbook for the Revolution. A special tribute issue in memory of James Simmons, who died last year, will be coming out this autumn. So treat yourself to a copy. And if you have problems obtaining it, please demand it from bookshops (who stock far too little local poetry) and if that fails, contact me through NBCAI and I will rush it to you.

Magazines

Black Mountain Review,
c/o Niall McGrath, editor
PO Box 9, Ballyclare
BT30 0JW
bmreview@totalise.co.uk
(quarterly literary journal)

Books Ireland
11 Newgrove Avenue, Dublin 4
Tel: +353 (0)1 269 2185
Fax: +353 (0)1 260 4927
E: booksi@eircom.net
(book review journal)

Fortnight Publications
81 Botanic Avenue
Belfast BT7
Tel: 02890 232 353
(political and literary magazine)

Irish Pages, Literary Review
c/o Chris Agee, co- editor
Linen Hall Library
17 Donegal Square North
(Irish literature journal with world perspective)

ILE, Ireland Literature Exchange
19 Parnell Square, Dublin 1
Tel: +353 (0)1 872 7900
Fax: +353 (0)1 872 7875
E: ilew@indigo.ie
www.irelandliterature.com
(Source for Irish literature in translation)

Women's News
109 -113 Royal Avenue
Belfast BT1 1FF
Tel: 02890 322 823
Fax: 02890 438 788
(Irish feminist magazine)

Publishers

Note regarding publishers: In order to save time, money and disappoint it is important that an investigation is made to ensure that the publisher is looking for material and that it is the right publisher for your work. For good advice check out the Salmon Press Frequently Asked Questions page or the Irish Writers' Centre websites. Good luck.

Beyond The Pale Publications
Unit 2.1.2
Conway Mill,
5-7 Conway Street,
Belfast BT13 2DE
Tel: 02890 438 630
Fax: 02890 439 707
E-mail: office@btpale.
(political and cultural interest)

Abbey Press
24 Martello Park
Craigavad County Down
BT18 0DG
(poetry press)

Blackstaff Press
Wildflower Way
Apollo Road
Belfast BT12 6TA
Tel: 02890 668 074
Fax: 02890 668 207
E: info@blackstaffpress.com
(fiction, poetry, non-fiction)

Lagan Press
PO Box 110
Belfast BT12 4AB
(poetry, fiction, non-fiction)

The Summer Palace Press
Contact: Kate & Joan Newman
The Summer Palace Press
Kilbeg, Kilcar
Tel/Fax: +353 (0) 73 38448

Poetry Press
Dedalus Press
24 The Heath
Cypress Downs
Dublin 6
Tel: +353 (0)1 4902582

Gallery Press
The Garden Lodge
Lough Crew
Oldcastle
Co Meath
poetry, drama
Tel: +353 (0) 49 41779

Also, local community newspapers will often print poetry from within their own constituency.

139

Biographies

Eileen Burke is a 41 year old housewife. She has never submitted any poems before as she just does it as a hobby. She has three daughters - 23, 22, 16. She is single now and enjoys writing poems about whatever comes into her head.

Olivia Butler was born in Belfast and has lived there all her life. She is married with three children. She was educated at Aquainas Primary School, St. Dominic's Grammar School and St. Mary's University College. She taught English, Drama and French in Cross and Passion Girls' Secondary School for a number of years but left when her own children were very young. She has never gone back to full time teaching but acts as a substitute in various primary and special needs schools. "I have always loved poetry and in between all my other activities I snatch some time to write poetry and short stories. I have a great affinity with Belfast and despite all its troubles I have no wish to leave it."

Noreen Campbell was always interested in writing and wrote her first poem as a child about a pet dog. Most writings were nonsense poems and written as a form of fun. She joined a creative writing class in 1995 in Shalom House. The encouragement she received from the tutors at BIFHE was super. She has had two poems and a short story published in *Abracadabra*.

Dessie Carabine started writing just over two years ago. His inspiration came from a local landmark on the Black Mountain called 'The Hatchet Field.' "What pushed me into writing about the The Hatchet Field *(Not only in God's Eye)* was the fear of someone else writing about it first. So I jotted down a couple of lines then I expanded on it and, low and behold, my first poem was born."

Deirdre Cartmill received an Award from the Arts Council of Northern Ireland in 2000. She was short-listed for a Hennessy Award in 1999 and has been a finalist in the Scottish International Poetry Competition. She has been published widely in magazines and journals including The Sunday Tribune, Poetry Ireland, Fortnight, Flaming Arrows, The Irish News, Black Mountain Review and Women's Work VI, VII and VIII. She

featured in Poetry Ireland's Introductions series of readings in 1999. She is currently completing an MA in Creative Writing at Queen's University, Belfast. She has also published several short stories. She was a finalist in the Live At 3/Royal Liver Assurance Awards and was short listed for a Financial Times Management Essay Award. She currently lives in Belfast and works as a script development executive with BBC NI Drama.

Linda Collins is 40 years old, married with three children and one grandchild. As a mature student she graduated from Queen's with a degree in English and is now doing a 1 year teacher training course (PGCE). She has loved reading poetry since childhood and finds writing poetry very therapeutic.

Bernard Conlon was born in Glengormley, Co. Antrim in 1959. He tumbled into higher education, studying history and politics. He has spent most of his adult life in mainland Europe, but has recently been spending more time back in his native Belfast. He picked up a strong sense of history (and narrative) from his grandmother. A political writer and consultant, he has been active in a variety of culture and information projects. He is gradually going public with a few short stories and poems, which he sees as just another way of capturing history and expressing political ideas.

Mark Cooper has been writing poetry for five years. "A desire to write more than just happy birthday on cards to my first niece spurred my early efforts - Silly Snail, Bumbling Bumble Bee. The poems focus on elements of the natural world and are simply written, mostly humorous but at the same time they are accurate in their observation of subject. I also try to put across simple messages like 'don't bury your head in the sand', 'don't take people for granted'." To guide and drive his writing he produces short collections (usually 20 poems) that follow a theme and the seasons. So far he has written three such works *From Mountains to the Sea, Poems from The Flax Mill* and *See in Your Garden*. In addition to his poetry, he is writing a book called *Into the Mill*, the story of which follows an East German couple who come to live in Northern Ireland shortly after the fall of the Berlin Wall.

140

David Cullen, born in August 1969, lived briefly in Ballymurphy, West Belfast before moving with his mother Patsy and two brothers Adrian and Mark to the Ormeau Road where he has lived for some 25 years. He has two beautiful daughters, Molly 8 and Eve 7 and is soon to marry his long love Kerry. He dedicates this poem to the friendship of his 93 year old grandmother Nellie McGirr.

William Dalzell is retired and has been writing poetry for some years. He is an honours graduate of the Open University. This year he has produced a booklet of his poetry entitled *Intensive*.

Vincent Dargan is a freelance photojournalist based in the North of Ireland. For the last twenty five years and throughout the troubled years in his native city of Belfast, he has worked solely as an independent documenter of local history. The recorded compilations of his *Changed Times* real life stories, is complimented by his large collection of more than 20,000 photographic images which depict the 'every day' street scenes of the people and their past way of life in the 'Catholic Nationalist' and 'Protestant Unionist' areas of west Belfast.

Jacqueline Dickson-Thompson, poet and playwright has worked in theatre off and on for many years. First as an actor, then director. She went to Ruskin College, Oxford, before embarking on the job of writer. Currently working on a new stage play and *The Belfast Collection*, a project of words and visuals.

Maria Doyle started writing poetry in earnest two and a half years ago as a result of her recovery from a manic-depressive illness. She says she was incredibly average at English in school, and was only flavour of the month when an unsuspecting teacher read words plagiarised from *Baggy Trousers*. Having moved on from robbing other people directly she takes comfort from the fact it has all been said before, probably more eloquently, so say it anyway. She lives in Warrenpoint with her notebooks!

Padraic Fiacc was born in Belfast in 1924. His family emigrated to New York, but he returned to Belfast in 1946. His collections include *Woe to the Boy* (1957); *By the Black Stream* (Dublin, The Dolmen Press, 1969); *Odour of Blood* (Kildare, The Goldsmith Press, 1973); *Nights in the Bad Place* (Belfast, The Blackstaff Press, 1977); *The Selected Padraic Fiacc* (The Blackstaff Press, 1979); *Missa Terriblis* (The Blackstaff Press, 1986); *Ruined Pages* (The Blackstaff Press, 1994); *Semper vacare* (Belfast, The Lagan Press, 1999); and *Red Earth* (The Lagan Press). He has edited *The Wearing of the Black* (The Blackstaff Press, 1974). His awards include the Æ Memorial Award (1957); a major bursary from The Arts Council of Northern Ireland, and a Poetry Ireland Award in 1981. He lives in Belfast.

Margaret Finlay was born in Dungiven, living now in Belfast. She has been a member of the B.I.F.H.E. class tutored by poet Ruth Carr for the past four years and for two years at another centre. Her work was published in Abracadabra 2 and 3 and she received second and runner-up prizes in each. She is grateful to Poetry in Motion for the opportunity to read in public.

Morna Finnegan is thirty-one and has been writing poetry since her early teens. Although she has been writing for many years she has only recently begun to make her poems public, and has had some work published over the last year. She is in the process of moving from the city to the country, where she hopes to have more time for her writing. She is expecting her first child.

Tony Fitzpatrick was born in Belfast and still lives there. He started writing about 20 years ago and has been in various creative writing groups in the West of the city. He is married with six children.

John Galbraith is a retired Civil Servant living in East Belfast. He started writing poetry during 2002 at a poetry workshop run by BIFHE. This is the first time he has written poetry for reading outside the workshop.

Matt Garrett is 29 years old and married with a two-year-old daughter. He was born and has lived in West Belfast all his life and can honestly say that living and growing up in this part of Belfast has contributed hugely to his inspiration through writing. "Belfast's dark history is very capable of telling its own story, as a writer and poet I can but try to, through my experiences of growing up in Belfast parallel that dark history with words that make people smile."

141

Stephen Gharbaoui was born in 1965 on the banks of the River Lagan. An economics graduate and former accounting technician, he is now employed in North Belfast as a mental health care worker. "Writing affords sensitive people a therapeutic platform to express and understand the context of their experience." He regularly attends Arcadia Café poetry gigs and is Secretary of the Critical Mass Performance Poets Collective. He has been published in the *Spirit Glass Collection*.

Ray Givans has two poetry collections published, from Lapwing (Belfast) and Grendon House (Isle of Lewis). He has won poetry prizes in Britain, the U.S. and Australia and was the first recipient of The Jack Clemo Memorial Award for Poetry (London). His work is represented in the anthology, *Artwords - emerging artists and poets from Ulster*. Currently, Ray is short listed for this year's Hennessy Irish Literary Awards.

Colin Hamilton was born in Belfast in 1957. Colin studied physics for a few years after leaving high school, but has continued writing poetry since he was 19 years old. His work was first published in a local magazine Scorched Earth in the early 1980's and he has been involved in the Belfast literary scene ever since; in more recent years taking part in poetry readings at Arcadia café and at Bookfinders Café during the 1997 Belfast Festival at Queen's. Colin spent a few years in the USA, mainly in New York City, which gave fresh material for his work, some of which was published with the help of the Arts and Disability Award in his first book of poetry *The Emperor of SoHo* (2000). He now lives quietly in South Belfast.

Royce Harper has gigged extensively and published two booklets *The Giant's Breath* and *The Action of Waves*. He regularly performs at the Democratic Poetry Party at Arcadia Café', as well as hosts/produces 'The Artery,' an Arts/Literary review and music programme on Northern Visions Radio. He is currently working on a collection of epigrams *Maxims for The Misinformed*.

Gavin Hawthorne, born in Belfast. "After a period of time in England, I have returned to N. Ireland, completing a degree in English at Coleraine (UCC)." He is currently working on an MA in English (Irish Writing) at Queens. He has had one poem published, called *Steps in Trust* (included), in *Artwords*, an anthology of art and poetry from Ulster in 2001.

Lindsay Hodges was born in 1967 in Belfast, where she still resides. She studied English at Queen's University, Belfast before joining the NI Civil Service, working in a variety of posts. Having returned to creative writing seriously three years ago, she has been developing a novel, together with a number of short stories. Lindsay has been focusing on writing poetry for the last year and currently attends a poetry writers group in Belfast taught by Ruth Carr. Several poems have been published by Women's News and another is due to be published shortly in Fortnight Magazine. In March 2002, she won the Between The Lines Showcase for new writers that featured as part of the Crescent Arts Festival, with two poems, *Birds of a Feather* and *Cook Yourself Calm*. The second of these was broadcast on Radio Ulster Arts Extra.

Tom Honey is a senior citizen, a retired primary teacher who has had an interest in poetry over many years. "As a teacher I encouraged the children to try their own poetry writing. I myself have been writing over a long period and have had some success in poetry competitions and have had poems published in some publications. I write about people I know and places I love and about the woes and pleasures we all experience."

Richard Irvine is 31, and lives in Belfast with his partner Morna. Although he wrote prolifically as a teenager, it tailed off in university, until being rediscovered about a year ago one sunny morning in Belvoir forest. He writes mainly about nature, and enjoys poets such as Mary Oliver, John Haines and Wallace Stevens, among many others.

Rosemary Jenkinson was born in Belfast in 1967 and has spent the last five years teaching in Greece, France, the Czech Republic and Poland, and has recently returning to Belfast. She won the Northern Arts Short Story Competition 1998 and the Black Hill Books Short Story Competition 2001. She is a part-time craniologist, pub consultant and a member of Queen's writers' group.

Carolyn Jess was born in 1978 in Belfast where she still lives. Writing her first series of short stories at seven and later, at twelve, a poetry collection (with illustrations) entitled *Interesting Tales of the Obvious*, she has written many poems, novels and screenplays since. She has studied at Queen's University since 1997, graduating with a BA(Hons) in English and Classical Studies, as well as an MA in Creative Writing. She has worked as a photographer (in Sydney, Australia), piano teacher, actress, and film director and enjoys travelling, writing and shark diving. She is currently undertaking a PhD on Shakespeare in Film and hopes to shoot her first feature film in 2003, while working on a debut poetry collection entitled *Inroads*. Her poetry reflects her concerns with, and interests in, the issues of time, space, love, memories, circularity and linearity, as well as the spiritual, physical and pre-destined trajectories and thresholds that permeate mortality.

Sandra Johnston is a twenty year old student studying English at Queen's, about to enter her final year. She enjoys writing short stories. The Poetry Roadshow she attended - it was with Ruth Carr - encouraged her to write more poetry. "I have never considered publication since I never thought my work was any good but Ruth gave us all encouragement and more confidence in our work."

Mark Kennedy grew up in North Belfast. The Troubles inspired his early writing. At the age of eighteen he went to University in Scotland. "It was there that the most powerful influence on my writing emerged, mental illness. After two turbulent years I returned to Queen's University, Belfast, where I study History and Celtic."

Ruth Kennedy is a third year student at Queen's university in Belfast, studying English and Theology. She started writing poetry when she was sixteen, as part of an expression of her beliefs and feelings about some of the special people and places in her life. "Writing has given me a way to vocalise my fears, and to be able to empathise with others who share my experiences. I hope that my writing will help me, in my future life, to help others use their imaginations confidently and express themselves freely."

Michael Little grew up in Belfast, close to the river Lagan and in sight of the shipyard cranes where his father and grandfather worked. Mike has been writing computer programs for over 25 years but only began writing poetry in 2001. His poem *Light on the Lagan* was published in *You Can't Eat Flags For Breakfast*.

Joyce Macartney is a centre administrator for a Belfast Community project and is now at an age where she doesn't want to be reminded just how old she really is! As a mature student at Queen's University, she gained an Honours degree in Social Anthropology. "This hasn't been of any practical use to me in my employment as far as I've noticed but I enjoyed reading for it anyway. I love words and language so I enjoy writing for my own amusement (and sometimes to amuse others). It has never been my objective to get anything published before but I was surprised and delighted to have my work included in *You Can't Eat Flags for Breakfast*. It was most encouraging and has spurred me on to write more poetry more often."

Mark Madden was born in 1960, raised in North Belfast, Mark has lived in England, Denmark and Canada: returning to Belfast in 1996 and opening Arcadia Coffeehouse with his smarter wife Deborah. Since 1997 he has hosted the north's only regular open mic session, and many other cultural gatherings, in the coffeehouse. Mark has been performing and organising for over a decade, and hopes one day to become quite good at it.

Martin Magee was born in Belfast in 1952. As a young man he began writing short stories, articles and poetry, mainly as a pasttime. None were offered for publication. He stopped writing after after marrying due to family and work commitments. He began writing again four years ago, with numerous poems published in anthologies and magazines. He contributed two poems to Poetry in Motion's *You Can't Eat Flags for Breakfast*.

Jim Mawhirk was born and bred on the Ormeau Road. He married and moved to Carrickfergus in 1966. Two years ago, he took up writing poetry and drama attending workshops with BIFHE.

Betty McAlister wrote her first two poems after being in hospital. Others came to her in quiet moments at work. On a weekend course at Bristol University she learnt to write short descriptive and fictional pieces. Subsequent workshops and BIFHE courses taught her to experiment with form and tone and how to write on suggested themes. "A few lines can say so much."

Brendan McDermott was born in 1953 in Belfast. Brendan likes to frequent second-hand bookshops and buy old editions, particularly of poetry and history. "I've read a lot of Irish history, but how sad it is! But sometimes I love to get away from the bustle and could 'live alone in the bee – loud glade,' happily!"

Fred McIlmoyle began writing poetry as a teenager but the hobby was eclipsed by career pressures in aircraft engineering. There his writing was restricted to technical reports and engineering procedures. In his fifties the bug again began gnawing and this time it was given free range and he joined Holywood Writers' Group where the communal interest stimulated productivity, not only in poetry but short stories and articles. The Poetry In Motion Project was a welcome outlet for this rejuvenated interest.

John McKittrick was born in West Belfast in 1934. He was educated at the Boy's Model School, then privately at Orange Academy, Royal Avenue, Belfast. Matriculating in English and Maths from London University (Exter), he worked with the Ministry of Home Affairs in Northern Ireland until 1980. Retired and moved to Scotland, he has become a hotelier and publican.

Maria McManus "My friend is the type of woman who could go in to a second hand furniture store called 'The Very Thing', looking for a filing cabinet and coming out with a kitten instead. I am a bit like that." Writing interests...poetry, drama... starting the MA at Queens.

Axel R. McMasters writes "Half a century in and I'm still hoping to meet the fascinating character who calls himself ALEX. He seems to lead a more interesting life than mine. Often I am tempted to change my name from AXEL."

Jacqui McMenamin is a registered psychiatric nurse, mother, poet and creative writing tutor. She has run a creative writing group with clients at the low security unit at Tyrone & Fermanagh Hospital since Feb. 2001 and has recently completed a community development course. She has been published in various magazines and anthologies and recently won Cuirt Poetry Slam award in Galway 2002.

Gerard McSorley is a retired joiner. He has always enjoyed reading and listening to poetry being read, but this is his first attempt at writing poetry.

John Mercer was born and educated in Belfast, and retired eight years ago after 35 years in the teaching profession. He has also been an organist and choirmaster in several churches over the past 47 years. In 1960 he founded and directed the Belfast Operatic Company, and is now its President. He spends his time now, as well as being a freelance musician, organist and composer, in part time university tutorial work, and in school examinations. He has been writing poetry for many years. As well as having published a small anthology in 1998, he has work regularly published in some of the Small Press Poetry publications.

Paul Norman is a thirty-three year old writer, English by birth, who made Belfast his home in 1987. He has a background in cross-community drama spanning pre and post cease-fire Belfast. He counts Ted Hughes, Emily Dickinson, Stevie Smith and Murray Lachlan Young as his literary influences. This is the first public submission of his work.

Christine O Reilly was born in Belfast and has been writing for ten years. Her stories have been broadcast on local radio. This past two years Christine has been with Conway Mill writer's group and is currently involved in the publication of a book as part of the Mill's twentieth anniversary. Christine began writing poetry last year and is amazed that her words have been included in The Lonely Poets' Guide.

Cian O'Neill is a freelance journalist, writer and painter. He is 25 years old and is now studying at St. Martin's Art College, London.

Catherine O' Sullivan was born in 1936 in Co. Kerry, Ireland. "I learned to love and recite poetry in my family under the gentle promptings of my mother. I worked in education and social work for many years in Malaysia and Peru. It was only when I joined the Belfast Institute of Further Education last year, that I was inspired to write poetry." She is very grateful for the supportive atmosphere the class provides and the encouragement of her tutors and friends.

Denis O'Sullivan is in his late fifties. "I was lucky enough to have a couple of short stories published in a QUB literary magazine. Since then, I have been dabbling in short story writing for years just for my own amusement." Recently, he decided to get a little more active and he joined a creative writing class organised by BIFHE. As a result he has had a story accepted by Ireland's Own for publication in August this year. "The poetry writing has come about as result of some of the work we have done in those classes. I was very surprised to find that I enjoyed it, especially the greater freedom in form that modern poetry appears to offer."

Vivien Paton is retired and lives in South Belfast. She attends a creative writing group in the Falls library; She writes short stories and poetry. She hopes to attend Ruth Carr's poetry group this autumn.

Robert Rainey is 23 and has written poetry for the last five years. He reads every month in Arcadia Cafe's poetry nights and has done that for the last 3 years or so. "The poems I entered for this competition explore ideas of de-romanticizing notions of 'Home'. This isn't to say I have an overly-cynical view....but a healthy dose helps...rather I admire the thought of honest communication in all respects the creation of true points of contact."

Maura Rea first began, like most people, at school where she enjoyed writing both stories and poetry. She was chosen to read two of her poems on radio but never kept it up past school. "I never intended to get into writing at all. However about three years ago I became involved in a Read to Succeed course in support of my local primary school. A requirement of the course was that I should write an essay or children's book - I choose the book and I was hooked. I was so delighted with the work and the piece itself that I enrolled in a creative writing course followed by a poetry editing course where I found that poetry is my forte and my joy."

Janet Shepperson was born in Edinburgh in 1954, she came to live in Belfast in 1977 and has worked as a trainee journalist, community service volunteer, administrative assistant, primary teacher and creative writing tutor with children and adults. She left full time teaching in 1985 to concentrate on writing. She has published many short stories, with two short listed Hennessey Awards, and poetry in Trio 5 (Blackstaff, '87, with Dennis Greig and Martin Mooney), A Ring with a Black Stone (Salmon, 95) as well as many journals and anthologies. "I try to divide my time fairly between writing, giving workshops and raising my daughter."

David Smylie is a single father and also a teacher. He has been writing poetry off and on for the past four years. He would like thank The Democratic Poetry Party: A loose collection of Belfast poets who meet on the first Friday of each month in the Arcadia Café. "Here I have found support, inspiration and friendship among kindred spirits."

James Snoddy thinks he was the only one in his class who could not write a poem. Unexpectedly and without any reason poems started to come when he was forty two years old. "I still cannot write to order". Quaker by birth, he published a book entitled Peace Poems, Family Poems and Others in 2000 to raise proceeds for the Ulster Quaker Service.

George Sproule was born and grew up in East Belfast where he has lived all his 43 years. His parents are from Donegal so he has a great affinity for that part of the world. He is a graduate of the Open University and has worked in the Voluntary sector for about 15 years. Before that he was in the civil service. He is a keen hill walker and musician (frustrated rock n' roller!). He is married to Christine and has one son David.

Pat Taylor writes mainly about her country childhood - its beauty and hidden violence. Born in Belfast in 1932, she left there at the age of nine, returning at nineteen. Her first poem was written about her husband after his death in 1984. But it wasn't until three years ago, when attending a class at Queen's that she began to put together a book of poems for her family, illustrating them with old photos. Her work has been published in Gown and The Honest Ulsterman.

Carolyn Thompson has always been interested in books and poetry and writing, but two and a half years ago, she took a weekend writing course and came away with two very important things - a bit of real encouragement and the good advice to join a writers' group. "For me, it was the real starting point. It gave me the impetus I needed to begin to work at writing poetry. It's very important to me."

Shelley Tracey is a South African who has been writing since she was five years old. She is inspired by the people she has met in her ten years in Northern Ireland, and by the wonderful local scenery. Shelley's poems and short stories have appeared in a range of collections . Her ambition is to publish an anthology of her own poems.

Pat Turner, born and reared in Belfast, she has been writing poetry for 20 years on both humorous and serious subjects. Her work has appeared in various anthologies, including *Echoes from the East*, *Write to the Core*, *I Know a Woman* and *Abracadabra* 1, 2 & 3. She won the NIE poetry competition run by BIFHE in 1998.

Iain Campbell Webb has been writing poetry for some ten years. He has published poetry, both in Ireland and England in various literary magazines, and his work has appeared in a number of anthologies in both countries. He has given readings of his work at festivals in Belfast, Dublin and England.

Una Woods first published work (both poems and short stories) in the New Writing Page of The Irish Press, edited by David Marcus. A novella and short stories, entitled *The Dark Hole Days*, was published by Blackstaff Press in 1985. Poems, prose-pieces and stories have appeared in anthologies which include *Wildish Things*, published by Attic Press; *The Phoenix Book of Irish Short Stories*, edited by David Marcus; an anthology of Irish stories published by Syracuse Press, USA; *The Hurt World*, edited by Michael Parker, published by Blackstaff Press. Her play, *Grace Before Meals*, can be seen at The Old Museum Arts Centre, Belfast, in December.

Jani X is a mother, singer, poet, homoeopath and scaredy cat who yearns for fulfillment. She began performing poetry in pubs, with Derry based 'Bunch of Chancers' poetry group, since then she has read in Galway, Belfast, Paris and New York. In 2000 she won best performance at the Between the Lines showcase and also won an Organic Award for Music, with her funk/jazz band EWF.